KELLIE'S BOOK

(with pics)

CARY GREGORY

To order additional copies of this book, contact:
Xlibris LLC
1-888-795-4274
www.Xlibris.com
Orders@Xlibris.com
551282

In loving memory of my daughter Kellie . . .
we didn't get near enough time

PREFACE

This poetic biography explores the heart and soul of a father who has, without warning, lost his only child. Ranging from joyous and uplifting to heartbreaking rhymes, this special book is created from a compelling desire to share the blessings of a wonderful daughter and her all-too-brief period here as a daughter and a mother. Inspiring as she was, she never lost hope of aspiring to and realizing her personal dreams. Many touching memories are shared in these poignant rhymes as elation and turmoil are explored. They lend credence to the positive effect she had on the people she met and, in essence, give a voice to her in immortalizing her existence.

TABLE OF CONTENTS

The

Muse

Has

Landed

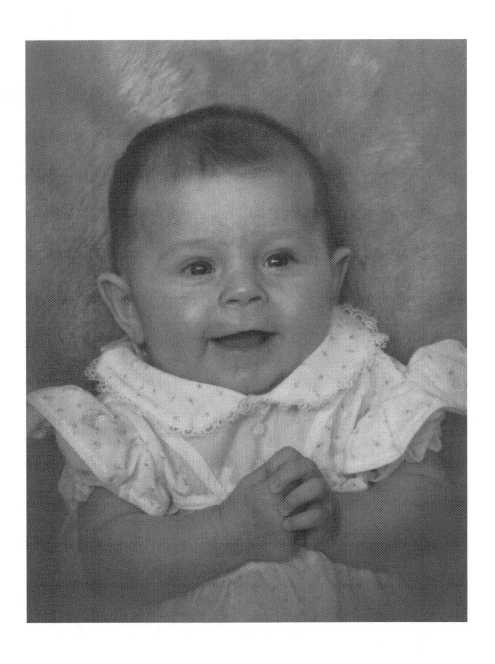

MY NEW PRECIOUS BABE

I realize it's early;
too early to know
about precious Kellie,
and how she will grow.
She's not even crying,
not 'cause she's asleep.
She's perfected cooing
with barely a weep.
The fact she's transformed me
and touched me in ways,
I hope to find knowledge
in the coming days.
So bring it on, Kellie,
my new precious babe.
He sent you from Heaven
to be here so may-
be you'll have some issues
with your hips or arms.
But nothing will phase me.
You're filled with such charms.
I've waited for years,
but now I am glad.
I'm so looking forward
to being your dad.

TWO HEAVENS (KELLIE'S SONG)

I know there are two heavens
and one is in the skies.
But when you run up to me,
the other's in your eyes.
You're such a special angel.
You're surely from above.
And with you here beside me,
I live my life with love.

CHORUS
Oooooo, I love my little girl.
She's everything to me.
If I should ever lose her love,
who knows where I'd be?

You're so alert and charming.
Your favorite word is "go."
I always feel such happiness;
the truest I'll ever know.

CHORUS
Oooooo, I love my little girl.
She's everything to me.
If I should ever lose her love,
Who knows where I'd be?

Whenever I feel worried,
you puzzle at my frown.
Touches from your tiny hand,
and I'm no longer down.
Your smiles to me are tender
and then you call me "Dad."
You warm my heart and then come smiles;
the most I ever had.

CHORUS
Oooooo, I love my little girl.
She's everything to me.
If I should ever lose her love,
who knows where I'd be?

You see I love my daughter,
so love your children, too.
Children are such special gifts;
they're all from God to you.

Kellie was not even two years old yet, but I was inspired to write this song about her. She was very special and I had no idea she would inspire me in numerous ways for many years to come.

KELLIE RAI GREGORY

Kellie Rai Gregory—
the apple of my eye.
You're always so sweet
and you never lie.
You're always so cheerful,
even when you're sick.
I've never figured out
how you accomplish that trick.
But just being with you,
it means, oh, so much;
like tickling your tummy
and feeling your touch.
You're cute as Cinderella
with wit and charm to match.
I'm sure when you get older,
you will be quite a catch.
Your heart is so warm
and filled with such love.
God lives in your heart.
You're sent from above.
My life has been blessed
since that glorious night,
when you were first born
and I held you tight.

The most important thing
I want you to do
is never forget that
I'll always love you.

This was an early poem, before the rhythmic flow kicked in. So while I may update some poems or add to them as the muse sometimes suggests, I am happy to keep this one in the form Kellie was told.

KELLIE—THE EARLY YEARS

Asleep in my arms, I quietly rock
my new baby Kellie, in jammies and socks.
She's light as a feather, at least so it seems;
this blonde green-eyed daughter has fulfilled my dreams.
She loves to be cuddled whenever I'm home;
especially on Sunday, she's never alone.
She entered a contest at eight months of age,
and won a nice trophy as she left the stage.
I hope she'll be proud of whatever she's done.
I'm thankful and proud. Next month, she'll turn one.
We played the game "Tickle My Belly" at two.
I couldn't find anything I'd rather do.
We later played "My Side" when she was just three.
I felt that she wanted to be with just me.
I take her to places. It matters not where.
She dresses so nicely and brushes her hair.
She makes me laugh, cry . . . does all this and more;
now that my daughter just last week turned four.
She just started preschool and does what I ask.
She's confident handling almost any task.
Now I'm so thankful, so glad I'm alive.
She's even more lovely now that she's five.
She brings warmth and love to shine on my soul.
She's done it for years 'cause she's six years old.
Her favorites are Superman and the tooth fairy,
Olivia, Elvis, and Mariah Carey.
And she says her prayers to God up in Heaven.
We've planned a big party for when she turns seven.

You suffered a few weeks ago with the flu,
but here is a line that really fits you:
"I love pink and green, but not orange or blue."
Kellie, I'm so proud of all that you do
It's wonderful being your daddy, my dear.
We encourage laughter and even a tear
with "Love You Forever" or watching TV
and movies like "My Life;" especially "E.T."
You've given me so much to look forward to.
I promise you, sweetie, I'll always love you.

This was an ongoing poem that was years in the making with just a few lines of thought each time. I envisioned an extremely long poem spanning her whole life, but it wasn't meant to be. Perhaps a full-length one is in the future.

I CAN'T MAKE MY LIL' GIRL CRY

If my daughter Kellie just called me one day
and said "I love you, Daddy. Come over and play."
I'm sure that I'd tell her "Be there right away."
I can't make my lil' girl cry.
When she was a baby, the doctors all said
"If she won't stop crying, then keep her in bed."
But man, are they crazy? They're touched in the head!
I can't let my baby girl cry.
If my little Kellie joined me in a store
to pick up some milk and bread, but no more,
I'd buy her a doughnut, a cookie, or four.
I can't make my lil' girl cry.
If my daughter needed attention one night,
and asked me to drop everything in sight,
you might think I wouldn't, but I'm sure I might.
I can't have my lil' girl cry.
If my precious daughter, one day after school,
in all her excitement, forgot a home rule;
I might use time out, but I'd never be cruel.
I can't make my lil' girl cry.
If Kellie decided she didn't want food,
and it was because she was in a sad mood,
I'd talk with her, tickle her, make her feel good.
I can't let my lil' girl cry.
If I thought one evening that I'd play a trick,
but she wasn't laughing because she was sick,
I'd call up the doctor and take her there quick.
I can't let my lil' girl cry.

As my daughter Kellie grows up more each day
and must solve a problem in her special way,
I'll guide her the best that I can and then pray.
I can't make my lil' girl cry.
You're thinking my daughter's a spoiled, little brat?
And she needs a spanking instead of a pat?
To see how you like it, I'll smack you like that.
And then see how YOU like to cry.
I'm teaching my daughter to be filled with pride
and I will continue 'til the moment I die.
For too many years, those spankings were tried.
We gained nothing to make children cry.

So much has been said about "spare the rod, spoil the child," but I was never a believer in that. Kellie was a well-mannered child and very deserving of all the love and attention she received.

MY DAUGHTER IS SIX

My daughter is six and she's better than fun;
so why try imagining her as a son?
I've taken her fishing—climbed mountains—thrown balls.
As long as I'm with her, she will try them all.
She's good with her artwork; does so well in school.
She's always polite although others are cruel.
She knows all her letters and numbers so well.
Share a secret? She'll promise never to tell.
She's good on her bike. She stays up on her skates.
I seize every moment to reiterate
there's only one girl I'd give everything for.
That's Kellie, my daughter, my friend, and much more.

By this age, Kellie had developed her wonderful personality and was already a favorite of teachers at school. She was well-mannered and dependable. I made several surprise visits to her there because she was an absolute joy to be with.

TO KELLIE

You're the apple
of my eye.
You make me laugh
but never cry.
Your voice is soft
and words are warm.
You have at least
a million charms.
You fill my soul
and thrill my heart.
I promise you
I'll never part.
I'll always love you,
this I vow;
but it's your bedtime.
"Kiss Me Now!"

This was actually the first poem I was writing with her next to me where she added the last line to rhyme. A very sweet memory.

LOVE YOU SO

My little Kellie,
how I love you so.
But you're not a baby,
'cause each day you grow.
You tap on my elbow
and raise up your arms.
You wish to be carried
and share all your charms.
And I can't deprive you.
That smile on your face
is lethal. Just ask and
we'll go anyplace.
We'll go to McDonald's,
buy toys at the store.
We'll rent "Ace Ventura"
for twelve times or more.
We'll play hide-n-seek 'til
we're ready to drop;
then play it again 'cause
it's no fun to stop.
You tell me you're hungry;
that you wish to eat.
So then from the kitchen,
I bring out a treat—

a fresh heart-shaped sandwich
of Jif and jelly.
But really I just want to
tickle your belly.
Oh goodness Kellie,
you're more than a dream—
the most wonderful, fantastic
person I've seen.
Remember each day,
I want you to know
how much your daddy
does love you so.

This poem is really self-explanatory . . . Kellie was the fulfillment of a dream and fun to be with. She was like an angel . . . always on her best behavior.

SWEET PRINCESS 1 & 2

Kellie, my daughter,
the Princess of Sweet.
Your teeth could rot out
from the candy you eat.

My darling, Kellie,
sweet Princess of Love.
You're blessed with such beauty
from God up above.
It starts with your long hair,
all shiny and blond;
the prettiest ever,
above and beyond.
It frames your cute face,
glowing, smiling, and soft . . .

    She loved being a princess at this age with getting dressed up for the contests. What little girl doesn't? This second one needed the muse to return . . .

School

Years

THE JUMP ROPE SONG

Over the waterfall and down through the woods,
came little Kellie just as fast as she could.
Leaping over logs and skipping over stones,
counting pretty flowers and naming her bones.
One, two, three, four, five, six, seven,
eight, nine. ten. Oh, there's eleven.
Ankle bone, calf bone, knee bone, thigh,
tail bone, rib cage, backbone. I
think I will jump out since I'm done with the song.
Who else likes to jump and wants to sing along?

I went to visit Kellie one day in grade school and saw her jumping rope at recess. Immediately, I got the idea that it could be fun for her to teach the other children a new song during recess. So during lunch at the table with her and some of her friends, I mentioned them singing while jumping rope. Their enthusiasm inspired me to write this simple song that encourages learning and coordination. Plus, names and gender are interchangeable, so it is practical and fun. It practically wrote itself while I was driving home. I taught it to Kellie and she shared it at school the next day.

IMMIGRANTS

So many immigrants—
they came from everywhere.
They braved the mighty winds and seas
and breathed the salty air.
They sailed their journeys on a ship
into the vast unknown.
They might arrive a family
or end up all alone.
The Germans landed by the thousands.
Neighbors called them "Dutch."
A talent to farm and low land costs
were what helped them so much.
They also built Conestoga wagons—
their canvas tightly-bound.
Farmers used these covered carts
to haul their crops to town.
Some came from northern Ireland
and they went farther west.
They built their homes up in the hills
and cleared the wilderness.
Others came from Sweden, France,
and picked a quiet spot.
The families were self-sufficient
'cause they worked a lot.

Farmers plowed and planted fields
and churned milk into cheese.
The mothers cooked and sewed warm clothes
so they wouldn't freeze.
They came here for a chance to live.
They came here to be free.
They came and settled for nothing less,
just like you and me.

This was another of Kellie's school assignments where she wanted to present a poem as part of her research. By now, many of her school friends knew her daddy enjoyed helping her write poems and looked forward to her reciting them. I enjoyed it primarily because I knew she had to do lots of research and it was more fun creating a poem than just another research paper. Getting an "A" for her work never bothered her, either.

WAVY

(done to the tune of Britney Spears' "Crazy")

Signals travel through space.
You know these signals as radio waves.
We move at the speed of light.
Now listen closely so you'll get it right.

You can't see us if you try.
We're here to help you understand why.

CHORUS:
    We're feeling wavy.
    Our troughs are deep.
    The noise we're making
    won't let you sleep.
    So o o wavy
    and our crests are high.
    Too many waves at once keep you up all night.

1873
James Clerk Maxwell thinking of me.
Later, while in Germany,
it took Heinrich Hertz to prove his theory.

We're so fast we can't be seen.
We're just vibrating raw energy.

CHORUS

X-rays, light, and microwaves
are radiation and measurable. We
have the lowest frequency,
yet longest wavelength that you will study.

We're so fast we can't be seen.
Now listen closely. You'll see what I mean.

CHORUS

♪

Kellie told me her school assignment was about radio waves. She was working with two other female classmates and we brainstormed. Again, research was extremely important and I suggested to her she could sing a song to the class with the research information. We made a tape of the song "Crazy" by Britney Spears and then found rhyming words to create the song. Her project partners were excited about the possibilities and we had the song written in no time at all. The three girls had a fabulous presentation and were rewarded with an "A." These special times with Kellie were what kept me even more enthusiastic about helping her anytime she asked.

LOST LOVE (THE BIRTHDAY SURPRISE)

The forecast was cloudy but no chance of rain.
He'd missed her six years and hoped now to gain
back some of the love and trust he'd once known.
From age nine to 15, she really had grown.
His stint in the army, because of a lie,
had weakened his hearing and sight in one eye.
He'd suffered a lot in his chaotic world;
but nothing compared to his little girl
and how much he loved her and needed her back
to accept him even after that vicious attack.
He'd left as a hero without fighting a war.
So handsome, he'd hugged her and walked out the door.
But once in the service, priorities changed.
It's like his demeanor was almost deranged.
He said yes to pills and poker and drink;
without taking time to just stop and think
how what was important was slipping away.
His split from his daughter grew worse everyday.
Her last letter to him cut right to the core.
He thought he'd prepared her, but she felt he tore
apart everything in her tiny world.
How could he be so mean to his little girl?
He then realized just how much he had lost
and vowed to regain it, whatever the cost.
Fourteen months of writing each week to his wife
finally earned him a new lease on life.
His wife wrote she'd meet him and even allow
his plans for the party. And true to his vow,

he came to his senses and severed the ties
of boozing and drugs with his army guys.
He blew up balloons, draped long streamers in trees,
set up several tables, and raked away leaves.
He'd planned it for months. All her best friends were there.
He'd given each detail the greatest of care.
He'd rented a limo and called up her school
to let her out early. She thought she was cool.
The limo was needed for birthday balloons
that she had been carrying with her since noon.
She climbed in the back seat. Her jaw dropped a mile
when she saw her father with his toothless smile.
Their six years of heartache fell straight to the floor
as they hugged each other. The past was no more.
As the limo driver turned into the park,
some black clouds were forming. But as it grew dark,
they renewed the love they had once both denied.
A truck out of nowhere crashed into the side,
throwing the father through glass and a door
amidst distant thunder. The deafening roar
of engines still racing was heard by a crowd.
They ran to the scene and gathered around.
The horrified father crawled through glass and tar
to get to his daughter, still trapped in the car.
He looked at her body as blood filled his eyes,
and knew she'd never get to her birthday surprise.

THE BRAT

Now let's see Mommy, you've turned 32
and though it's your birthday, there's still lots to do.
You need to fix breakfast, like sausage and eggs.
You're going out later? Then please shave your legs.
Now after the dishes—give Uncle a break:
fold up the clothes on the bed you should make.
Your room is a pig sty and smells really bad.
You clean it up now or I'm calling my dad.
And just for good measure, clean up your room, too.
There's only so much that my small hands can do.
And look at this carpet—there's dirt everywhere.
The weekend is here—change your underwear.
And that pile of laundry all over your room
needs to be washed. And where is the broom?
This vinyl floor lately severely needs mopped.
That must be completed before you can stop—
just long enough, missy, to fix us some lunch;
like sandwiches, ice cream, bananas, and punch.
Now after we've eaten and dishes are done,
there's still more to do before you have fun.
That horrible smell coming out of the pot—
needs sanitized whether you like it or not.
And I need a toy. My room's full of junk.
So cancel your plans with whatever hunk.
And when we return and if I'm satisfied,
we'll both play a game I've been dying to try.
Now you be my slave and I'll be your High Queen,
and you don't stop working 'til everything's clean.

Mom, I've been teasing. This isn't the way
that I really feel. Have a Happy Birthday!

Kellie was such a blessing and so well-behaved that it was harmless fun to imagine if things were the opposite. Kellie wanted to give her mother a poem for her upcoming birthday, but also wanted it to be funny. With our sense of humor, this was hilarious. It was so over-the-top, you couldn't help but see the humor in it.

ONE DOWN, ONE TO GO

I said I'd send a poem,
or maybe, I wrote "two."
But since I've been so busy,
I'm still at none for you.
I'm up before the rooster
to always greet the sun;
and thank each of my lucky stars
if I'm in bed by one.
A steady stream of clients
is always calling us.
We could cut back our hours,
but hey, who needs the fuss?
We finish what we promise
as quickly as we can.
And sometimes work together
if needing extra hands.
But trips up to Missouri
and with my favorite girl,
are what I truly treasure—
my best times in the world.
This poem's such a struggle.
Who knows when I'll be done?
Hey wait! These words are rhyming.
I guess I'm left with one.

MOTHER, I OWE YOU

The neighbor's long letters tore into my soul,
as life for me spiraled out of control.
    Jesse was seven. Her brother was five
    when their father left with his final goodbye.
    Twelve years together no longer was worth
    the deep, mental anguish, the sorrow, the hurt.
    Her mom cried that evening, then swallowed her pride
    when she realized that she wouldn't hide
    behind the resentment and all of the strife.
    She still had a family and must regain her life.
    She sat down her children, and in her torn dress,
    outlined some strong rules to get out of the mess.
    But Jesse erupted. She loved her dad so,
    and hated the way her mom wanted to go.
    But she was just seven, and finally gave in,
    as her mother started all over again.

    The kids had to listen. A new plan was made:
    to make sacrifices and be less afraid.
    And church every Sunday and during the week
    was how she'd been raised, and therefore, would teach.
    They had to share chores and do all they could
    to work close together and payoff it would.
    They promised their mother to give her their best;
    to eat all their veggies and get plenty of rest.
    This worked a few years with all going well,
    but focused distractions can put us through Hell.

Jesse's impatience led her down a path
deserving, perhaps, of her sweet mother's wrath.
The poor girl was troubled and made her life rough.
She did miss her father and that made it tough.
She wanted the payoff . . . and wanted it now.
She made up excuses and twisted her vow.
As Jesse got older, she tested her mom
and dated some strange hairy doofus named Tom.
It's not that she loved him, but more like a dare.
She wanted attention and just didn't care.
Her mouth and hot temper she got from her dad,
and rarely respected the mother she had.
Her mom never quit, though; continued to show
to both Ben and Jesse, the way they should grow.
Unwavering kindness was sprinkled with love
and undying faith in the God up above.
It all still seemed crazy to Jesse. Indeed,
believe in a spirit in her time of need?

In one of his letters, which seemed strange to me,
was Jesse's own writing. Now how could that be?
He wrote that it must have been thrown in the trash,
or maybe an entry that she meant to stash.
But "Mother, I owe you" was written on top,
then followed with words that made my mouth drop.
    "I asked for the keys and to borrow the car.
    I said I'd get gas but not go very far.
    But youth and bad choices were on for that day,
    and put me in a very precarious way."

Along with the entry, her mother's reply
to some time uncertain, but still made me cry.
    "Just know that I love you in more ways than one
    for all that you stand for and all that you've done.
    Know I admire and respect you each day,
    but sometimes it's hard just to say it that way.
    I know I got angry and laid down the law,
    and it was a rather unfavorable flaw.
    But only for making it better, I swear,
    and you'll understand it's just 'cause I care."

Their words overwhelmed me, I wanted to quit,
but the neighbor's letter continued a bit.
    Still, there were times when they all got along
    with short trips together and singing old songs.
    That's when Jesse told her one day at the store,
    "Mom, you're so deserving of this gift and more.
    And it's in the past all my dumb petty crimes.
    I'm sorry I've let you down so many times."
    "Jess," her mom told her, "deep down in your soul
    is who you are truly. Give her the control.
    And always remember, whatever you do,
    you're my only daughter. I'll always love you."
    Sadly, that moment was fleeting for Jess.
    Her appreciation was short-lived at best.
    For her, to be thankful was like keeping score.
    "Mother, I owe you" was less like a chore.
    In fact, that became her new favorite phrase,
    playing on her mother's long working days.
    On prom night, Jess wanted to stay out 'til 4.

"I owe you one, Mother," she yelled out the door.
Even Ben said "Jesse's way out of line!"
His mom reassured him, "She's gonna' be fine."

The neighbor's long letters had me overwrought.
I still couldn't see past the battles I'd fought.
Poor Ben and Jesse had been through it all;
both being abandoned when they were so small.
Jess racked up a tally, and it barely clicked
when she heard her mom was severely sick.
But never repaid her, and on Christmas Eve,
her mom passed away from a heart disease.
God had allowed them just 18 short years,
to become a family and face all their fears.
I went to the funeral to pay my respects,
with only ideas of what to expect.
I hadn't seen either of them in so long,
and felt that whatever I said would be wrong.
Upon seeing Jesse, a few feet away,
she said to herself, but I heard her say:

"Mother, I owe you for all that you did—
working two jobs while raising us kids.
Never complained of the hand you were dealt.
Proving each day the love that you felt.
Mother, I owe you for all that I was,
for doing the things that a good mother does.
While we were a handful of problems, you still
taught us the value of love that fulfills.
I owe you so much 'cause through all of my years,

you guided me gently and calmed all my fears.
You'd always reward me for trying my best.
I never felt like it was part of a test.
I guess your priorities were always the same.
That's how 'Mom, I owe you' turned into a game.
You never insisted the payback be good,
'cause it was a game, and you understood."

I couldn't believe the insight this girl had.
She hadn't, after all, turned out so bad.
She then walked up front, and standing with Ben,
spoke just to her mother while we listened in.

"How can I thank you for all that you've done . . .
for teaching us all of the dangers of guns?
You said cut with scissors instead of a knife,
and showed us you love us each day of our lives.
Even as babies, you kept us from harm.
I've so many photos of me in your arms.
As you showed me things in this beautiful world,
I felt like I must be the luckiest girl.
I'm sorry. At age 15, I was so trying,
you sat for hours worrying, waiting, and crying.
And I misplaced things that I had just bought.
I sure wasn't living the way I'd been taught.
Your kindness, compassion, for all that I did . . .
I didn't deserve it when I was that kid.
I sometimes thought you should be harder on me.
But it wasn't your nature. You shared that with me.

Mother, I owe you for what I've become,
although I went too far with 'second to none.'
I wasn't ungrateful, but I didn't see
I should focus on others instead of just me.
But it's not your fault. You did all you could.
My friends were just telling me 'Don't be so good.'
But if, as teenagers, we were that smart,
God wouldn't have given us moms from the start.
You started as 'Mom,' but became my friend.
I just never thought THIS is how it would end.
Mother, I owe you for all that I am
and helping me choose a good-hearted man.
You taught me to manage, but you'll surely be missed."

Then she laid down the rose that she'd softly kissed.
This girls heart was breaking. Of that, I was sure.
But her mom had given her strength to endure.
'Cause 30 years prior, in my perfect life,
I'd chosen her mother as my only wife.
I thought how our lives are all webs that we weave
and felt so uneasy, I wanted to leave.
What Jesse had said, I shouldn't have heard.
Still, I found myself listening to her final words.

"Mother, I owe you for all this and more,
for love and support without keeping score.
You taught me so much—what life's all about.
And how to get through it if ever in doubt.
You taught me that Heaven is where we will be
and there I'll repay all that you gave to me."

Like most of us children, we come up way short
in thanking our parents for all their support.
I failed both my children and even my wife
when I gave up on what's important in life.
She'll never forgive me. I'm sure Ben is mad.
They both deserved better from a loving dad.
Coming to grips with this reality,
I feel lost forever. I'll never be free.
My God, she was seven, and Ben barely five.
Would they want to know now that I'm still alive?

This one took 14 years from start to finish. These characters were
the opposite of anything I was living, but I was sadly aware of similar
circumstances that many families were going through. Kellie was always
appreciative that her father loved her enough to make her a priority. As
with many of the endings of my poems and stories, I am often just as
surprised as the average reader is.

JEN'S FAVORITE PILOT

He'd been a pilot seven years. He'd always loved to fly.
He then met soulmate Linda and they couldn't say goodbye.
They married eight months later on a roller coaster ride.
When baby Jennifer was born, the father beamed with pride.
The many flights were tough on him. He loved his baby so.
But he would sing these words to her each time he had to go.

"If you start to miss me and think I'm not around,
I had to fly off somewhere while you're safely on the ground.
But when you really need me, you needn't look that far.
You'll always find me deep within your heart."

He chose to fly out less and less, anticipating when
he'd cherish special times with Linda and their daughter Jen.
His wife and Jen grew closer, but Jen idolized her dad.
So he would always sing this so she wouldn't be so sad.

"If you start to miss me and you think I'm not around,
I had to fly off somewhere while you're safely on the ground.
But when you really need me, you needn't look that far.
You'll always find me deep within your heart."

The night before her birthday, Jen received some awful news.
A father's plane went down and had police looking for clues.
The wreckage was discovered, but his body wasn't found.
So Linda bought a casket and they buried it in the ground.
As it was being lowered, Jen looked up toward the sky,
and heard the words her father sang before his last goodbye.

"If you start to miss me and think I'm not around,
I had to fly off somewhere while you're safely on the ground.
But when you really need me, you needn't look that far.
You'll always find me deep within your heart."

Kellie was such an inspiration in many facets and just preferring her imaginary friend to be called Jenny was inspiring to me. This one again, just flowed out effortlessly and was written in mere minutes. This was also one of many that caused her sentimental tears.

JENNY AND HER LITTLE PET WHALE

Listen everyone while I tell a tale
about a girl named Jenny and her little pet whale.
Early one morning after eating a peach,
Jenny put on her swimsuit and went to the beach.
She found an old bucket for castles of sand.
A boy walked by and said they look grand.
She went to a surf shop and rented a board;
then jumped in the ocean and tied on the cord.
After surfing for hours, she rested awhile;
then she awoke to a killer whale's smile.
Shivering, frightened, and sweating from heat,
she wondered was she what he wanted to eat?
The black and white whale, though, didn't attack.
He leaped from the water to land on his back.
Off in the distance, a rainbow appeared
and Jenny, she smiled and wiped at her tears.
She realized this blackfish had meant her no harm.
She'd made a new friend and reached out her arm.
She swam to her surfboard and climbed up on top;
then laughed as her friend did a big belly flop.
The hurricane waves made surfing more fun.
They shared the whole ocean in the Florida sun.

Still with amazement, the board at her side,
she pitched out the rope and hopped on for a ride.
The whale put the end of the rope in his teeth,
and pulled Jenny along at a very fast speed.
A few surfers yelled. A crowd gathered then
to watch the girl surf with her awesome friend.
With one final splash, he washed her to shore.
She glanced back around; the whale was no more.
Everyone there on the beach clapped and cheered
when they heard how Jenny overcame her fear.
To Jenny, the hero was really the whale.
That's why I decided to share this great tale.

For a school assignment, a vivid imagination was needed. Since I
had recently completed "Tania and Her Pet Whale," Kellie asked to use
it as a basis for her poem. She always loved the name Jenny, and worked
hard at rewriting Tania's adventure.

A. LAVOISIER

Summertime, 1743,
a baby was born to make history.
He lived life in France,
and had a romance,
and spent his life studying chemistry.

By the early 1770's,
chemists and scientists struggled to see
how chemicals react
when under attack.
The problems were in their theories.

This chemist's name was Lavoisier.
He experimented everyday
with matter and things
that couldn't be seen.
The mass is unchanged, he would say.

In his laboratory, he discovered this—
a theory that most others had missed.
Matter was not made,
but it could be weighed.
He shared this with his wife, then they kissed.

To show the Conservation of Mass,
he heated some tin in a glass.
No weight lost or gained;
the tin then looked stained,

and a scientific law would be passed.

He proved this Law of Conservation.
This law would spread throughout the nation.
Other chemists came;
they wanted the fame.
This law would make up a foundation.

But then the political state
would summon a large magistrate.
Science was schooled;
a judge overruled,
and a guillotine chop sealed his fate.

To this very day, we look back
at a theory that we all would lack,
if not for Lavoisier
and his thoughts that day.
His papers are now proven facts.

    This was another of Kellie's attempts to turn a research paper into a poem. Again, I was proud of all the research she had to do to help make a nice poem from the facts and be rewarded with another "A."

Fun Times

KELLIE RAI

(melodic section)

Dad   - Kellie Rai, you watch entirely too much TV.
Kellie - **Daddy, you know I can't live without my "Jeannie."**
D   - Kellie Rai, you need to clean up all your messes.
K   - **But Dad, I can't. I want to try on my new dresses**.
D   - Kellie Rai, you need to help me set the table.
K   - **Dad, I can't. I'm watching all my shows on cable.**
D   - Kellie, what's with all the bread sticks and the pizza?
K   - **I was hungry, Dad. I paid it with your Visa.**
D   - Any clue when you think these bills will be stoppin'?
K   - **I don't know but right now I need to go shoppin'.**
D   - Kellie, didn't you swear you would do some bakin'?
K   - **Dad, I did! I made a pop tart. You're mistaken.**
D   - Kellie Rai, you need to finish all your homework.
K   - **I will, Daddy, when I hang up on this phone jerk.**
D   - Don't you know when you go out, I always worry?
K   - **If I'm not home by 4 am, I'll try and hurry.**
D   - Kellie, what'll all your friends say when they see you?
K   - **They'll say "Whoa Mama, gosh, I wanna' be you!"**

(chorus section)

D   - Kellie, there's no way you're going out like that.
K   - **OK fine. I'll need some money for a hat.**
D   - Kellie Rai, you need to put away your toys.
K   - **Dad, I will when I'm done talking to these boys.**
D   - Kellie, you know that's not what I had in mind.

K	- **It's OK, Daddy. Chill. I'll be fine.**
D	- Kellie Rai, you need to study hard in school.
K	- **Daddy, please. I'd rather hang out by the pool.**
D	- Kellie Rai, you need to help me clean the floor.
K	- **Daddy, why? I helped you once when I was four.**
D	- Kellie, please go wash your hands. It's time to eat.
K	- **I smell liver. There's no way I'll eat that meat.**
D	- Kellie Rai, behave and change your attitude.
K	- **Dad, you know I'd rather sit and watch "Hey Dude."**
D	- Kellie, please. I can't keep going on like this.
K	- **Daddy, shhhh. I'm trying hard to reminisce.**

Kellie and I shared lots and lots of fun times over the years. She loved to watch "Full House" and I had no problem with the wholesome TV show. The Olsen twins became hugely successful with their movies and the song "Stayin' Cool" became one of her favorites. Borrowing that melody, I created some typical parental remarks and Kellie had fun with the answers.

AMY AND GLENDA

I asked Kellie, Tuesday, where she'd like to go.
I suggested the park, but she replied "No."
She wanted to play at the Fun Zone instead.
When I mentioned her scooter, she nodded her head.
We packed up the scooter and I grabbed my skates.
I knew that our time was gonna' be great.
We weren't there five minutes when a small boy got hurt.
Then Kellie said "Daddy, sugar-babe alert!"
The dark-haired young woman, dressed in black and white,
was really attractive. I said "Kellie, you're right."
The daughter was friendly, and wanted to play
with my daughter Kellie, so I said OK.
I trusted my daughter to play nice and then
when we swung together, they also joined in.
We sang very loudly and had lots of fun
and how time had flown 'cause where was the sun?
Reluctant to leave, it was a safe bet
we'd see them again—the two we'd just met.
Nothing prepared me for later that week,
when there at the park, again we did meet.
I thought that our chances to see them was slim.
It'd been just two days since we'd seen them.
Greeted with smiles helped put me at ease,
though I'd come from work with paint on my knees.
We sat on the bench and talked for awhile.
It feels good to close the day with a smile.
She asked for my number and I now have hers.
When we get together, it'll be fun. I'm sure!

LATER . . .
A couple new friends we seem to have found—
a pretty young mother and her daughter the clown.
The mother is Amy and seems very nice,
but hey, it's still early. We've only met twice.
But in those two times, we've talked quite a lot,
so future park meetings will be a sure shot.
As far as a date thing, it's not a big deal.
Although Amy does have a lot of appeal.
It's just I'm not looking for a special someone.
What matters the most is that Kellie has fun.

This poem was a prime example of how easy it was to meet someone or take Kellie somewhere and be able to immediately write about the experiences. I had no idea at the time how important and revealing all these poems would be in our later years. But they seem to serve as moving pictures captured forever. They are like paper videos. Best of all, I could share my words with Kellie at later times and she would automatically remember additional things that happened from her point of view.

A TRIP TO DISNEY

I could've worked the weekend and made a lot of cash.
Instead, I packed up Kellie, and made a hasty dash
northward to Orlando to meet up with a friend.
Gene brought his two small daughters and his sister Jan.
Kristen is the youngest and Kelly's now a teen.
And Jan, his older sister, wow, she still looks 18!
I'd made my reservations and guess it worked out right.
Rooms so close together would've kept them up all night.
We hit the park quite early and took in lots of rides—
a few a little scary, but we calmed the girls' cries.
A bit odd seeing Janice who spoke less when we were young.
And then to get a photo of her sticking out her tongue!
A long parade of neon passed, then things got a bit rough.
The massive crowd of rushing people caused us to split up.
Gene said he wasn't worried as they drove back to the inn.
But Kristen and Jan hit the sack at maybe 10 past 10.
We headed for our favorite ride once we did all we could.
We stood in line to hop aboard the coaster made of wood.
Then at the stroke of midnight with our log paused at the top—
rushing waves and flashing light launched our 5-story drop.
We flew like in a rocket shooting down through the abyss.
It sure was fun—Splash Mountain—the ride we'll always miss.
On Sunday, we hit Epcot for another day of fun.
It was foggy in the morning, but then out came the sun.
The body waves—FANTASTIC! The 3-D shows and more
seemed more fun than I remember when I was there before.
I gotta' admit . . . it was a blast—the time spent with the girls.
I hope we all can plan it again—a trip to Disney World.

LETTER FROM ONE B AND COOKIE

Hi Kellie! It's One B and Cookie's here, too.
We wanted to write a letter to you.
The last couple days while you were at home,
we stayed here at Campbell's to play on our own.
We missed you, of course, but knew you'd return,
so there was no cause for any concern . . .
Wait a sec, One B! I've something to say.
Hi Kellie! It's Cookie, this glorious day.
I'm sure One B told you we went to the park,
and saw lots of boats and heard some dogs bark.
We also played outside awhile in your tent.
He played Superman while I was Clark Kent.
But did he remember to mention to you
about the two kittens—and what they were up to?
It seems these two kittens, named Tabby and Tom,
had come to the park to play with their mom.
They're not far away. They live up the street,
and come to the park like three times a week.
But when we were there, they asked us to play
a ball game called "Sniffle and Whiffle Away."
Though like Whiffle Ball, instead, we used yarn,
like that time we played up in Grandpa's barn.
We sprinkled the ball with catnip and spice,
and with their mom there, we had to play nice.

Tom was my teammate and ran really fast.
I thought we would win, but they caught us at last.
The score was still tied when we left at nine.
Maybe you and your dad can join us next time.

This poem was inspired because Kellie and I had gone to one of my client's homes for a weekend and she had forgotten her two stuffed animals there when we left. It was not a local home so it was going to be several days before I could go back. I did not want Kellie to be sad without her favorite stuffed animals, so I delivered this "letter" to her so she would feel better and know they were doing just fine.

WHOSE CAKE IS IT? (3 Acts)

Cast: One B, Cookie, Cousin Jed, Lello Bear, Gizmo, Barbie, Ariel, blue & white cat (cameo)

(credits are displayed while piano plays tune)

ACT ONE:

ONE B'S HOUSE, AS IF LOOKING THROUGH LARGE PLATE GLASS WINDOW OF LIVING ROOM—DAY

A busy ONE B (koala bear), is singing quietly and humming to himself, straightening up the room
The phone rings

ONE B
Hello? Oh hi Gizmo. What's up? Yes, I was on the phone earlier. Why? He can't? Well, thanks for call . . . Oh, you will? Yes, yes . . . that would help me out a great deal. I need the ice cream definitely . . . and some fresh bananas if they have them.

A knock is heard at the door

ONE B
Listen Giz, thank you so much, and yes, that would be fine. Someone's at my door so I need to go. OK, thanks again. Bye. (crosses to the left to answer the door)

ONE B
Hi Cookie. Come in, come in.

COOKIE enters.

COOKIE
Hi One B. I tried calling but the line has been busy. Is everything OK?

ONE B
Oh yes, of course. I'm just trying to get everything together for this afternoon. I haven't gotten the cake start . . . Oh, Giz was just on the phone. He said cousin Lello was feeling really tired and couldn't go to the store.

COOKIE
Oh, I'll go. What do we need?

ONE B
Thanks, but Giz volunteered. He said he could bring the stuff by in awhile.

COOKIE
That's great. But that was mainly why I stopped by. I know you are busy. Is there anyway I can help?

ONE B
Well, let's see. Here's my checklist. Barbie and Ariel are wrapping the gifts right now. Cousin Lello picked up the candy yesterday. I hope he feels better this afternoon in time for the party.

COOKIE
Yes, he told me last week how excited he was about today. Maybe I can go over and see if he needs any soup or medicine . . . that is, if you don't need any help.

ONE B
No, Cookie. That would be good for all of us . . . and I'm sure he would appreciate it. But I am fine here. I just need to get started on the cake.

COOKIE
OK then. I'll see you this afternoon at the party.

(Both cross to the left)

ONE B
OK. See you then. Bye!
(to himself) OK, now to get back to baking. (crosses right and out of sight) Hmmm, where is that cake pan?

(Knock is heard at door)

ONE B
(loudly) Just a minute! Who could that be? (crosses to left) Cousin Jed! How are you?

(They hug)

COUSIN JED
I'm fine, fine. I know I'm early. I hope it's OK. I would've called from the bus station but . . .

ONE B

No, it's great to see you. Come in. Come in. If you want, just take your stuff down the hall. It's the second door on the left. I was just getting ready to bake a cake. (exits offstage to kitchen)

COUSIN JED

A cake? Mmmm . . . whose cake is it?
Phone rings

ONE B

(offstage) Ah . . . just a second. Hello, this is One B.

COUSIN JED

(shrugs a moment and exits offstage to bedroom)

ONE B

Oh, hi Cookie. Cousin Lello is feeling better? That's wonderful. He'll be by later? OK Uh huh Uh huh Yeah Yeah Yeah Yes, of course, and tell him Cousin Jed just got here. Yes, several days early, but I am glad he's here. OK, see you later! (hangs up phone) (loudly) Jed???

COUSIN JED

(offstage loudly) I'm in here. (enters stage right) The room looks very nice. Thanks again for letting me visit.

ONE B

Oh Jed. It's wonderful to have you. We are going to have a great visit. Plus, you're in time for the party. It's this afternoon and I still need to bake the cake. (moves toward kitchen)

COUSIN JED
Great! I love parties. Whose cake is it?
(Knock is heard at door)

ONE B
(exiting offstage) Um . . . Please get that, would you? (voice trailing) I need to get in the kitchen right away. (exits to kitchen)

COUSIN JED
But . . . OK, I'll get it. (crosses left) GIZMO! How ya' doin', ol' buddy? Yummy, that ice cream sure looks good!

GIZMO
(enters with boxed ice cream)
shakes and makes noise

COUSIN JED
Yeah, I just got in awhile ago. Wanna help me unpack? One B's in the kitchen making a cake.

GIZMO
(moves toward kitchen)
shakes and makes noise

COUSIN JED
Yeah, me too. Say, whose cake is it?

GIZMO
makes noise
(exits stage left)

COUSIN JED
Whose? OK, I'll start the unpackin'. (exits right)

END OF ACT ONE

ACT TWO:

ONE B'S HOUSE, BACKYARD (cardboard scene)—EARLY AFTERNOON

ARIEL and BARBIE are sitting at table making party decorations. ONE B enters from back of house.

ONE B
Girls, these are looking great. I am having Jed and Gizmo come out here to hang streamers and blow up balloons. If you want to go in and put your magic touches on some desserts, that would be fantastic.

ARIEL & BARBIE
(in unison) We would love to!
(they stand up and exit into back of home)

(One B stands at table momentarily, and then also exits back into home)

PLAY CONTINUES . . .

    This was a play/puppet show I wrote to basically surprise Kellie on her birthday. I worked out voices for some of her favorite toys and since Gizmo just made noises, he was the one who kept telling the other characters who the cake was really for. Since Kellie's birthday was a few days away, she had no clue it was all for her. I put a lot of effort into this unique gift and pretty much winged the rest of it. Since it was actually early evening when I started it, ACT 3 had dark rain clouds which allowed me to turn out all the lights and have Kellie close her eyes. While my recorded voice and music kept her attention, I went to the kitchen and quickly brought out her lit birthday cake while the characters were singing in unison "Happy Birthday." When we sang HER name, she opened her eyes to her party.

HOUSESITTING 1 & 2

I've written some poems with humor in mind.
It's no fun being serious all of the time.
Now just remember—these rhymes are just jokes
to help bring some laughter to all of you folks.
Been sitting for days watching this place.
My eyes are bloodshot and there's beard on my face.
The switches don't work and the A/C is shot.
I don't use the oven 'cause the fridge is so hot.
I sit here for hours with nothing to do.
The mirror invites me to play peek-a-boo.
No one comes over. No one ever calls.
Did I really promise to be here 'til Fall?

Housesitting for you is no problem, you know,
but I'm getting anxious for winter and snow.
Been up for two days and still can't get no rest.
You've been robbed three times—but I'm doing my best.
Kellie guards the house while I'm watching the yard,
but we're both so sleepy, I should hire a guard.
We had a dog once and it worked out awhile;
then a thief brought some steak, and the dog smiled.
I'm here on the beach, but I ain't seen the shore,
'cause I stay so busy. I've no time to snore.
My truck blew the engine, so I'm stuck here alone.
Darline and Kirby, <u>please</u> come back home.

MY SWEETHEART, SCHNOOKUMS-POO HONEYBUN

You tell me you're thrilled it's your birthday again.
You're not five or six, but instead, turning ten.
While some are astonished at how time has flown,
me—I'm just happy at how you have grown.
"Cause I still remember your short stubby toes
and patiently wiping your red runny nose.
The crib was so lonely, I cradled you tight
and rocked you to sleep on those long restless nights.
It wasn't much later when you started walking,
and soon after that came the gab . . . I mean talking.
I'd sit next to Mommy—that you couldn't bear.
You pushed her aside just so YOU could sit there.
I've always loved music and dancing with you
became, rather quickly, a fun thing to do.
Responsible work often took me away,
but I would make good by the end of the day.
I'd missed you so much, I put all else aside;
got down on all fours, and gave you a nice ride.
The time we spent learning was seldom enough,
and saying goodbye—gosh, that always was tough.
But our bond grew stronger, and I was so pleased
you kept on insisting to spend time with me.
We searched out some places we could call our own
like Circus World—Mirtha's—Discovery Zone.
You even had Santa come by several years,
although his first visit, you greeted with tears.
You did well in preschool. To keep you from harm,

I disciplined Andrew and squeezed Michael's arm.
Let's see—that all happened at the Learning Pond.
I became your hero and strengthened our bond.
We've seen Mississippi and stopped by my dad's,
where you've claimed has been the most fun that we've had.
Well, other than Blizzard Beach at Disney World.
I've never seen a wetter, more satisfied girl.
I'm never bored with you. Look forward each day
to being together—at home, work, or play.
Liked going to Fanti's and chipping up tile,
or watching Kim with you if just for awhile.
Now doing your chores was another matter.
Do dishes—play Barbies—you'd choose the latter.
You know I'm just kidding. I helped with the chores,
so when you had playtime, we had time for more.
I look back at all of the things we have done,
and your good behavior was second to none.
You've done well in grade school. I'm proud where you stand.
I try to encourage all A's when you can.
And then YOU'LL be proudful and understand why
sometimes I'm so happy, I can't help but cry.
It's your birthday, Kellie, so have lots of fun;
my little sweetheart, schnookums-poo honeybun.

This phrase just came out one day, and Kellie loved it. To be impressed with her or proud of her was an understatement. She really did have a sweet heart and adapted well wherever we went.

ODE TO OLIVIA

I've written lots of songs and poems before,
but never one this long to one I adore.
At just age 11, I first heard your song
"If Not For You" playing and my heart was gone.
Your voice mesmerized me and filled me with glee,
but nothing prepared me for '73.
They said you were country. OK, that was fine,
but Dolly and others were left far behind.
You earned "their" awards for a couple of years,
and I was so happy and cried joyous tears.
"I Honestly Love You" was your top hit to date,
and earned you a Grammy and man, it was great.
I started a diary at around age 14,
and wrote about places and people I'd seen.
While I shared events that happened that day,
I listed your songs the radio played
and even included, when later at home,
your albums I'd played while I was alone.
Collecting your stories, I told all my friends
that you were the best and would be 'til the end.
I bought up your posters, watched you on TV
like "The Midnight Special" and "Donny and Marie."
It's funny. I'd haul hay with friends until late;

but if you'd be singing, then we'd stay awake.
I watched all your specials like "Hollywood Nights,"
admiring your talents, your hairstyles, and tights.
I saved all your pictures from teen magazines,
'cause you were the loveliest woman I'd seen.
I had to have records and those 8-track tapes,
then dub to cassettes and they all sounded great.
I loved how you sang, your accent and all.
No one in my eyes had stood quite so tall.
I saw you in concert when I was 16,
and sat there in awe . . . fulfilling a dream.
You emerged from the curtain, (Paul W. was done),
in a sexy green jumpsuit that was second to none.
I taped the whole concert, from beginning to end,
and since then, have played it again and again.
At just 17, I became a DJ
and got to choose most of the songs I would play.
A rather small station, but I didn't care.
It meant I could broadcast your voice ANYWHERE.
The station was country, which I thought was cool,
plus getting requests from my friends at school.
So your songs got played, like four every hour,
except when I worked at the transmitter tower.
I got to read "Billboard" once the news was done,
and often worked night shifts until about one.

I got all wrapped up in my job playing songs,
it caused me to slack off and sometimes do wrong.
Instead of a grounding for coming in late,
my parents would take my recorder and tapes.
But I straightened up, and at the year's end,
I noted positions your songs would come in.
I'd listen to Casey, and while it was fun,
I'd think what a waste if you weren't number one.
I miss all the countdowns with you at the top.
I know you love singing, so why did you stop?
And what's happened to your new "Gaia" CD;
where you portray life as a goddess from Greece?
And speaking of "Grease," ha, when I was 18,
your outfit of leather was out of a dream.
I watched every showing and learned every line.
I snatched up the poster 'cause you looked so fine.
Even my mother joined me for a show.
The language was raunchy, but how could I know?
Then two years later, you did it again.
I saw "Xanadu" with a few of my friends.
The day that it opened, I saw every show.
Some friends asked me over, but I told them no.
Your acting in movies, like "Two of a Kind,"
but especially "Grease," leaves others behind.
I've not seen "Toomorrow," but hope to someday,

and can't put a cap on the money I'd pay.
With your acting talents, you'll always get hired.
So close to perfection, you'll never get fired.
Mister Reed, stuff your "If white bread could sing . . ."
He's worse than a critical dip ding-a-ling.
Your "Greatest Hits" package and "Physical," too,
became two of the biggest hit albums for you.
I've saved all your clippings—like thousands so far.
If someone tried stealing, I'd be no-holds barred.
They're filed away daily; their condition pristine.
I probably have some even you haven't seen.
I really like "Soul Kiss," and "Heart Attack," too.
I also look forward to lyrics by you.
"Changes" was one that you wrote years ago.
Maybe you're writing for your next show.
I feel in my heart you've been working toward
another American Music Award.
I share you with Kellie and it's such a kick
when she sings your songs and catches on quick.
Cartoons you hosted, "Hallmark's Timeless Tales,"
are so hard to find. But with the details
of clippings I have from my TV Guide,
surely they're good since you did them with pride.
A positive model in whom we should trust
since Earth conservation to you is a must.

My sibling has met you out there in LA.
Your clothing's included where she spends the day
at Nordstrom's. She watches the girls as they sew,
making sure shirttails don't hang down too low.
But for promotion, you scheduled a date
for autograph signing and had to stay late.
Since you signed to me, but started with "K,"
Kellie got one, too, at the end of the day.
Back in October, some years ago,
I finally met you, but not at a show.
You came up to Boca for a tennis event,
and I bought two tickets—money well spent.
I thought about Kellie, but she couldn't come.
At just three years old, I thought she's too young.
But I videotaped as much as I could
and shared it with Kellie. It turned out that good.
Another time listening to Casey's countdown
to see who had earned each decade's top crown,
the 70's listed you at #4.
But then we got "Physical" and "Xanadu" scored.
You finished "Top Woman" of the 80's decade
from all of the movies and records you made.
And then you did movies and shows for TV
like "A Mom for Christmas" aired by NBC,
and three episodes of "Snowy River."

Your acting and singing still made me quiver.
"Christmas Romance" finished high on the charts.
I wish you'd do more instead of so far apart.
I mean, every few years is way too much time
to wait for your movie, but suits you just fine.
So I'll patiently fill the gap with your songs,
and even ask Kellie to come sing along.
Films like "It's My Party" and then "54" . . .
just you being mentioned made me want the score.
"Essential Collection" means ALL your LP's,
and 8-tracks and singles, cassettes, and CD's.
I've found early records, like "The Biggest Clown,"
and they are uplifting if ever I'm down.
But it couldn't help me hold back countless tears
when I heard the news. After all of your years
accepting awards of platinum and gold,
your musical comeback was now put on hold.
I heard of your cancer and sent you some cards.
I'm thrilled you are better, but sure it was hard.
I remembered the day that Elvis had passed.
It saddened me deeply. I'd hoped he would last.
I knew I was worried I might hear the worst,
but you were a fighter and put your health first.
Still, just 44, surprised as could be,
but thrilled you emerged from your surgery.

To come to CA was a big dream of mine,
but loved more your singing in June '99.
I even had Kellie for the week long trip.
She got front row seating to see Daddy flip.
Your wonderful concerts in the Sunshine State,
have not been recorded, but still sounded great.
I've proven I've followed your career down the line.
You're probably wondering where I found the time.
When something's important, especially like this,
there's not a split second that I would've missed.
Conquering struggles, you strove to soar high.
If God granted wings, I'd swear you could fly.
The greatest role model I ever hoped for
for someone so precious I love and adore.
When I put my daughter to bed late at night,
I turn down your music and turn out the light.
I never did drugs. I don't even drink.
I don't need that nonsense in my life. I think
as long as I'm rearing my daughter with pride,
she'll love and respect me and stay at my side.
She worships me now like some superman,
and gives me more love than I'd ever planned.
I never fight with her. We're always in sync.
It's only through God we've forged such a link.
And my admiration for you now lives on

in my daughter Kellie through your gift of song.
I'm so glad your daughter has someone like you
to honor and cherish and love what you do.
Congrats go to you for your many awards.
What ones have you lately been working toward?
I realize you probably just do what you do;
you reap what you sow, so it comes back to you.
I'd do anything to write you some tunes,
so we'd show up Whitney, and then Debby Boone.
But if you're retired—the limelight is out,
then I understand. But there's still no doubt;
if you ever wanted your stardom to rise,
you'd shoot to the top and sit high in the skies.
'Til then, all the best to you, yours, and career.
Have a great Christmas and a Happy New Year!

Olivia was a major influence in my life and I was proud to share her with Kellie and have her validate the admiration. They shared many characteristics like kind-heartedness, generosity, and respect for all living things.

MY MUSE

I sit here inspired. I'm almost in awe
of what I have written—the poems and songs.
Been writing for hours, or so it seems,
of everyday fantasies, pleasures, and dreams.
They've all made me laugh. I've had lots of fun.
I feel like they're some of the best work I've done.
But I can't leap up for some pats on my back,
if you're still asleep, and no need for a plaque.
I've written of people and places to eat,
and what they might say the first time they meet.
I don't think I've said how much you're my muse.
If given a choice, you're still who I'd choose.
I don't force the words. I just let them come,
but use a thesaurus to help me with some.
I've written 'bout hosting a TV talk show
and how one prepares it from the word "Go."
And what it would be like to make the crowd roar;
and suits say "All right!" as the ratings would soar.
Just mere speculation is all this has been,
while you're sleeping soundly with your buddy Jen.
But I'm out of ink and my bedtime's done passed,
so I'd best get going . . . but it's been a blast.

LET'S GO!

I woke up one morning and I rubbed my eyes.
I looked out the window to see the sunrise.
My parents were sleeping. I looked at the clock.
It sat at 6:13. Oh my, had it stopped?
I didn't feel tired. I felt wide awake.
I guessed that my parents were sleeping in late.
If 7:00 was when we were needing to leave,
I'd borrow Dad's jacket with long, fuzzy sleeves.
I looked in the mirror and brushed back my hair,
and then I kissed Mommy and Daddy right there.
Mommy kept sleeping, but Dad rubbed his cheek,
and hugged me to thank me for being so sweet.
"I've got to get up and get ready for work."
"But Daddy, you promised." He felt like a jerk.
He called up his client and said "Later, dude."
I looked at my daddy and said "My, how rude!"
He laughed. He'd been teasing and knew all along
of our plans to travel. He'd done nothing wrong.
We fixed us some breakfast as quiet as we could,
and then brushed our teeth like everyone should.
We didn't wake Mommy as we locked the door.
I looked at my watch. It said 6:54.
While driving to Naples, I reached for my tote.

Inside was a giant, inflatable float,
and a long rope Dad said he could attach.
We shared a few brownies, but had a whole batch.
I also saw gators along the roadway.
I counted way more than 100 that day.
Dad said we'd have fun and we'd do many things—
that there was this place he called Bonita Springs.
"We're getting there early. Our options will be
I'll have time for you and you'll spend time with me."
When we hit the beaches, we had a great time.
I'll tell you about it next time in my rhyme.

Bonita Springs was a place on the west coast of Florida that turned out to be a great spot to vacation. It was somewhat secluded and the perfect size for us. If you arrived early am, you could set up the whole area as if it was your own. We always enjoyed our times here, even if the birds did get carried away at times.

MY NEXT RHYME

I promised a poem in my last "Let's Go!"
But once I'm done eating my fresh sloppy joe.
Ok, dinner's over and I will try hard,
but know our vacation was megastarred.
I felt like a princess with all that we did;
another advantage of being a kid.
I'm sure that my daddy shared all the news
and all the fun things we were going to do.
We sat up a table with our food and stuff;
and ran to the ocean 'cause I'd had enough
of small swimming pools and no waves at all.
We stayed the whole day and we had a ball.
No exaggeration was needed that day.
I laid on the raft and just floated away.
Daddy stayed busy with all of my needs,
but mostly just busy while laughing with me.
If ever a daughter had reason to gloat,
other kids wanted to ride on my float.
His creative thinking and great attitude
made me quite willing to show gratitude.
I feel really special when Dad has free time.
Leah may want him, but this daddy's mine!

FAMILY REUNION (. . . for Tyanne)

Four years ago, when I was here last,
I said I'd return 'cause we'd had a blast.
All the great food and fine fellowship
had made the short time a well-worth-it trip.
So it seemed a breeze to try it again;
to brave thunderstorms and drive through the rain.
We stopped in Orlando, three hours from our house,
to ride on Splash Mountain and see Mickey Mouse.
We took off again, dusting cars as we passed,
avoiding the cops 'cause I was driving so fast.
Jeez, I'm just teasing. With Kellie in the car,
I'm not gonna' speed, but we had to drive far.
We hit Mississippi—a sight to behold
'cause driving those miles was really getting old.
We got to Grenada, checked into the inn,
and then placed a call to some of our kin.
We shared many laughs and played a few tricks,
especially when they came in and I acted sick.
Tyanne and Gary dropped their voices low.
I was so proud of Kellie as she played her role.
I was really surprised. She wasn't half bad.
I jumped up and then they both knew they'd been had.
They took us to dinner at the Evergreen
and the buffet was bigger than any I'd seen.
Kellie chose shrimp and I ordered some wings,
while Tyanne was daring and tried everything.
They showed us the sights while it rained cats and dogs.
I glanced back at Kellie asleep like a log.

The next day we drove to the Jenkins' home.
I wished I had purchased some deep carpet foam,
'cause Kellie played outside and then tracked in mud.
I felt lower than an ant blown up by a Scud.
But this is the South. They forgive things like that.
Or do they? For lunch, they charged 80 bucks flat.
And then they arrived—Tyanne's young sons.
With spiked hair and earrings, they both carried guns.
No, I'm just kidding. They weren't very loud,
and Tyanne and Gary should be very proud.
You could say I teased them—once, maybe twice,
but they were good boys. Kellie said they were nice.
But wait! I'm getting way ahead of myself.
I'll rhyme a <u>few</u> kin, but not everyone else.
We got to the schoolhouse, but couldn't play games,
'cause it was still locked. But I won't name names.
I shook hands with Horace and hugged Aunt Clyte,
but quite a few people were staring at me.
I told them "Relax, you're not being conned.
I came years ago. Remember James Bond?"
I introduced Kellie and she was a hit,
but still I was wishing that we'd done our skit.
I even sat down at the keys for awhile,
but jazz or Beethoven weren't really my style.
The family meeting went quickly this year.
When stomachs are growling, it is hard to hear.
But Kellie and I had more talking to do.
Grandma's sis was there and Tyanne's mom, too.
I'd spoken of this highly since Kellie was three,
because of the kindness they'd all shown to me.

I'd hoped to see Grandma whom I hadn't heard from,
but Grandpa had fallen, so they didn't come.
Neither did Linwood, Lavon, nor Lavere—
these are Mom's brothers I'd missed through the years.
The ones that did come were really a riot.
If you're blood-related, you really should try it.
There's lots of great foods and plenty to drink,
unless you crave beer—they don't serve that, I think.
But getting together is what we're there for—
to update our lives, share memories and more.
The food's just a bonus—like icing on cake,
and with Tyanne's cookbook, there's lots you can make.
We stayed one more night and thanked them a lot;
and stashed a crisp 50 back under their cot.
Then we headed back to the Florida sun
to develop our photos and relive the fun.
So all things considered, the trip wasn't bad,
because we're here safe and "I love my Dad!"

Kellie was only 7 years old at this time, but always a perfect lady with me. There was a lot of joking around with my relatives because Kellie and I were pretty convincing and they knew it was all in good fun. But it really was a fantastic trip and I cherished these times with Kellie. She played along and always enjoyed the attention. I was thrilled that Kellie shared my sense of humor and she wanted the last phrase here to be hers.

**FIRST EVER SHOCKING PHOTO
OF SPACE CREATURES**

HOMAGE TO THE BUFFSTER

Down the dark smoky alley
or out behind a tree,
lurks a mean scary monster
to folks like you and me.
Its hands can rip your heart out.
Its eyes can pierce your soul.
Unless you're heir to Superman,
your fate they may control.
But while us lowly pagans
struggle through each night,
we can't begin to fathom
the demons Buffy fights.
While safely in our bedrooms
drifting through our dreams,
a hero dressed in leather
fights amid bloodcurdling screams.
She doesn't want your pity.
She doesn't like to fight.
But she's the Chosen One
and she does it 'cause it's right.
So if it's late one evening
and you hear the rustling grass,
well, if you make it safely,
it's 'cause Buffy saved your a**!

(alternate endings)

So if you're out one evening
and hear sounds strange and new,
it just may be the Buffster
looking out for you.

If you're out alone some night
and hear sounds strange and new,
get your butt in gear.
There's a monster after you!

She may be kissing Angel
or have a thing for Spike.
But Buffy's got you covered,
no matter who she likes.

"Buffy, the Vampire Slayer" was an awesome show and also a pretty cool board game. Kellie admired Sarah Michelle Gellar as Buffy and we shared some great times. Cutting her teeth on "Buffy" at such a young age kept her from being afraid of scary movies later in life. I was glad she could sit and enjoy them rather than being too scared to watch.

TANIA AND HER PET WHALE

Everyone listen while I tell a tale
of a young girl named Tania and her pet whale.
You need to be quiet. You have to sit down
in a chair, or the floor. Just gather around.
Now early one morning after eating a peach,
she put on her swimsuit and went to the beach.
She'd finished her chores and had time to play,
but went there alone that warm summer day.

A hurricane coming brought waves crashing in,
and she put on lotion to cover her skin.
She found an old bucket for castles of sand;
a young boy walked by and said they looked grand.
She oiled up her surfboard from the beach shop nearby,
then put on sunglasses to help shade her eyes.
She surfed several hours, then laid on her board,
and the vast blue ocean she drifted toward.

She woke with a start when a wave hit her brow,
and sat up in fear as she looked all around.
Surrounded by ocean, no shoreline in sight,
she knew she must paddle if it took all night.
She knew by the sun which way she should go
and then started kicking. She knew it'd be slow.
All of a sudden, without any clue,
a huge killer orca jumped out of the blue.
She fell off her board, surprised at the sight,
but reached for the rope as she filled with fright.

The waves hit her face and stung at her eyes.
Poor Tania was scared and started to cry.
She thought of her father and mother at home,
and knew they'd be worried she went out alone.
Shivering, starving, and sweating from heat,
she wondered was she what he wanted to eat.
The dark moving clouds that covered the sky
spelled impending doom. She thought she would die.
The menacing orca, though, didn't attack.
He leaped from the water to land on his back.
Off in the distance, a rainbow appeared
and Tania, she smiled and wiped at her tears.
She swam to her board and climbed up on top,
then laughed as the whale splashed a big belly flop.
She realized this mammal had meant her no harm,
but maybe protect her. She reached out her arm.
Relieved, Tania thought, as she patted his back,
"Thank God I'm not his afternoon snack!"

The humongous waves made surfing more fun
as fears disappeared in the Florida sun.
Again several hours she spent on her board,
and then saw the shoreline and pointed toward
the place she called home, where loved ones did wait.
But she'd still remember her two-ton playmate.
Then with amazement, the board at her side,
she pitched out the rope and hopped on for a ride.
The whale swam to hook up the rope in his teeth,
and Tania hung ten at a very fast speed.
She'd learned how to balance while standing on sticks.

Her father surfed well and he'd taught her some tricks.
A few surfers yelled. A crowd gathered then
to watch this girl surfing with her awesome friend.
She cruised through the pipeline, then trimmed to the top;
then flew off the wave for a rad acid-drop.
Even the lifeguards sensed she'd be alright,
and stared at the unbelievable sight.

With one final splash, the whale washed her to shore.
She glanced back around, but the whale was no more.
Then everyone on the beach clapped and cheered
when they heard how Tania had conquered her fears.
To Tania, the hero was really the whale.
That's why she decided to share this great tale.
You ask since I tell this—how I know it's true?
'Cause Tania told me. You believe me, don't you?

With my daughter Kellie's encouragement, I sat down to write a poem about a pet for an upcoming Open Mic Night at a local bookstore. At the end of the weekend, this poetic story had come to life. It was always one of Kellie's favorites and we had agreed that it would make a great children's book. Since then, it has gone through a few minor revisions and was published. This is the latest version. No poetic biography book about Kellie and her many shared life experiences would be complete without including this poetic tale.

P. E. PLEASE

I went to school one windy day
with so much on my mind;
like clothes shopping, flip flops flopping,
and leaving Summer behind.
My Freshman year—exciting, yes,
to meet new kids at school.
But TV shows and staying up late
were way much more than cool.
Now books are filled with stuff to learn
and occupy your time.
And teachers do their best as the
steps to success you climb.
But I had better things to do—
have fun and socialize.
But those won't help my grades stay up,
nor hanging out with guys.
This was what my father said.
I fought it for awhile.
But as I saw friends make mistakes,
his wisdom made me smile.
I never liked sports all that much.
Well, Dad says skiing's fun.
I do like swimming in the pool,
but that's the only one.

Jumping rope has long since passed,
unless you're really fit.
Or have a special song to sing
to go along with it.
Then Dad shared some points with me
and suddenly, I heard
how health was more important now.
I analyzed each word.
So here at school in P.E. class,
I do all kinds of things:
climbing, running, playing games
that make my muscles sting.
And it's not really school at all;
it's now a thrill to me
to go to school, like everyday,
and have fun in P.E.

Kellie had never been a big fan of organized sports, but was always active with me. I wrote this from her point of view with a bit of parental encouragement.

HOME REPAIR HEADACHES

My rhyme about Kellie sent chills up her spine.
So, being impressed, she asked was it mine.
I answered it was and she said "Very good!"
I feel like I'd write everyday if I could.
Instead, I must work at repairing old homes—
fix doors, and check wiring to replace their phones.
It's up in the morning before the cock crows
and 'til late that evening, it's GO! GO! GO! GO!
In spite of my routine, well, being like that,
it's not even close to the depressing fact
that she lost her home. She's going through hell
by losing mementos and memories as well.
Moving to there and then back to here,
she's suffered a lot and I'm sure spilled a tear.
Refreshed, she awakens to greet a new day.
One ring from the doorbell and that quickly fades.
She waves to her husband. She drops off the kids,
and since she wants cool deck, she asks for a bid.
The subs test her limits and make the days hard.
"Who is that weirdo in my backyard?"
She kicks at the plumbing. She bangs on the wall.
How can one woman manage it all?
She's got the worst headache of women in Dade
when Dildo and Stumpey use her house for shade.

"My front door is ruined! Why is paint on my tile?"
Her girls "sassing" back may also get her riled.
Since I know her anger could raise a high tide,
when I'm in her house, I swallow my pride.
I work so she feels there's no reason to shout.
She's much too attractive to pull her hair out.
I'll try to stay cheerful and do what I'm told
and hurry to finish before we grow old.
Then we'll all be happy that glorious day—
I'll paint the last patches and she'll yell "Hooray!"

Just one of the many clients I had while in the construction field, and Kellie got to meet most of them. She was inspiring me to write and this client, Becky, was pretty impressed. She had three daughters of her own, but she saw firsthand how important Kellie was to me. I liked Becky and we became friends, but I was glad to finally know she had her house back.

JUST KIBBLES AND BITTS

Kibbles and Bits! Just Kibbles and Bits!
This stray cat would only eat Kibbles and Bits.
One cup of milk mixed with a half cup of dry
was all she was eating. Believe me, I tried
fresh Friskies and Whiskas, gourmet in a dish . . .
this cat wouldn't touch 'em. She wouldn't eat fish!
I bought all the flavors cats love, I suppose;
then tried Tender Vittles. She turned up her nose.
Now cats can be finicky. I had me one;
but I swore to keep her 'cause she would be fun.
I found this gray Persian; her tail was white-tipped,
while I was in college. My French class I skipped
to groom her and Spot was a most fitting name.
I ran her to Mom's when no one voiced a claim.
I Binged Persian cat breeds. Wow! My cat is blue.
So why only dog food? I found not a clue.
I went to my dorm. Our lounge was a huge mess.
The guys had been looking for coeds, I guessed.
Bill ran down the hall yelling he'd seen a mouse;
but he liked to party. He could have been soused.
With it near the weekend, I figured "Why not?"
The next day I drove home and returned with Spot.
The floor nice and quiet, the guys had gone home.
I relished me, Spot, and that mouse all alone.

I tried my room first and left Spot there awhile,
but she was so passive which hastened a smile.
In Bill's room, I petted Spot down near his bed,
then oops! There's a chapter that I haven't read.
I studied awhile before falling asleep,
and when I woke up . . . Ha! Dead meat at my feet!
Licking her paws just as proud as could be,
Spot knew what I'd wanted and brought it to me.
Since Bill had developed a friendship of sorts,
I couldn't imagine a better retort.
Monday in his backpack, Bill felt a soft lump.
He reached in to feel it, and man, did he jump!
I had some great times with that crazy ol' cat,
then wondered a bit when she got really fat.
Instead, Spot was pregnant—the first time in years.
Then quickly got sick and I fought back my tears.
She had just two kittens . . . and then called life quits.
No names fit them better than Kibbles and Bitts.

This was one of Kellie's sentimental favorites that also has been enjoyed by others. It is one of the "inspired trio" for my first Open Mic Night that Kellie encouraged and supported. In a shorter form, it has been published, but this is the variant in its revised entirety.

STAYIN' FRIENDS

He's proud of you, Kim, in more ways than one,
with all that you're doing and all that you've done.
He hoped that you would, and he's happy to say
he knew that you could if you tried to one day.
He's often quite busy, but glad when he phones
and when he asks for you, you're often at home.
He won't stop by often. He feels you need time
to arrange your priorities and get them in line.
Though you're often asking him for his advice,
is it 'cause he's brainy or always so nice?
Whatever the reason, your best is his guide
'cause deep down, he cares and that's simplified.
But it sometimes stings—some say he's too old.
Yet he was quite happy, the one day you told
him dating a guy about his same age
was fun; then you split up because of his rage.
You're not even 20. He's said all along
that you could stay friendly and that wasn't wrong.
You even met Kellie. You two laughed a lot.
But friends try to use you and take what you've got.
You're special to Kellie, and I like you, too.
But where is this going? It's all up to you.
He's never been spiteful and he's never mean.

You said he was worthy to be in your dreams.
He's bent over backwards without being paid.
He's dropped everything to come to your aid.
He hoped you'd discover through your ins and outs
that he was a fella' worth caring about.
Now he's been enlightened while being with you.
Would he care to date? I'm sure! You know who?
Just look in the mirror and you'll see her face.
He'd try anything and he'd go anyplace.
I'm sure that he's never felt this way before.
and doubt he's had someone to care about more.
But you left him stranded? YOU made the plans?
Well, he deserved better and can't understand.
But there's no regrets. What he did was true
and due to the feelings that he had for you.
You don't feel the same so it'll never work?
He won't hang around then and feel like a jerk.
He wishes you well. Let time pass with them.
You'll see the best guy was someone like him.

Kim was a friend of mine for several years and Kellie and her got
along extremely well. Many fun memories all three of us shared.

FUTURE PLANS

He's sitting there thinking what life will be like
coming home to a child, a dog, and a wife.
The child would be precious, devoted and true.
She'd do out of love what he asked her to do.
A dog would be faithful, happy and strong;
returning the love he'd stored all day long.
But how would it be coming home to a wife?
Would her heart be cold and words cut like knives?
Or would she have redeeming factors and more?
I guess there's no way to know really for sure.
But I must admit, in my last fourteen years,
the happiness I've felt has brought me to tears.
I dated three years, but knew all the time,
I'd stay with this girl and life would be fine.
And even my daughter, who adds to the mix,
was just being honest and not playing tricks.
We finally got married and we were so glad.
She's still to this day the best friend I've had.
Stayed true to ourselves and shared that respect
and so far, it's worked. We've not given up yet.
Our love runs so deep, there's never a doubt
in either of us what love is about.
And now with two kids and one on the way,
we're thankful and know we're blessed everyday.

So my wife and I will always be true.
We started as friends and then our love grew.
Mistakes from the past can be turned around
as long as you're planted on solid ground.
You call them mistakes . . . so why then repeat?
To do them again is accepting defeat.
Don't let such temptations alter your course.
Approach family dreams with a tour de force.
You can still sit there and ponder your life;
but true to yourself is how you'll get a wife.

This was just fun speculating, never intending to become reality. Hope the guy took my advice, though.

FATHER TO FATHER

When a gifted author takes a pen in hand,
all his vivid writings are known throughout the land.
He may toil and tarry for a better word,
but his mind rejoices when all his thoughts are heard.
In his books and poems, if he has the clout,
effortless emotions are what he writes about.
He may pick a subject, guided by a muse,
and the words flow freely, whatever he may choose.
He may choose his father, knocking on the past,
knowing time has limits, however long it lasts.
Or the muse can take him more to a sacred place,
where memories are golden and honesty is based.
The thing is, recollections of strong parental hands,
are written for that father so he might understand.
They're not to match with siblings, or even with a friend.
We all have different outlooks, and will have 'til the end.

When a father's caring, it shows in many ways:
taking time to make time, lengthening his days.
I can still remember, seeing "Santa's arm,"
swearing you were still in the chair all nice and warm.
Years went by before we all found out it was you.
Kellie even hugs me and still she wonders "who."
Music was important and sharing TV shows:
"Happy Days" on Tuesdays, Sunday nights—"Tom Jones."
We were always working—life's like that on a farm.
But you were always nearby protecting us from harm.
But my teenage highlight was, where you said "OK,"

"Olivia In Concert" blowing me away.
I barely had my license, but with close friends in tow,
you loaned me your tape player to help record the show.
And church was so important, we went three times a week;
and had to deal with strangers that called us "Jesus freaks."
I won't go into details; sometimes they made me sob.
But music was my calling and got me my first job.
Although I worked on Sundays—almost a crime back then;
it meant the whole world to me, so hardly was a sin.
And I remember, also, you took me on your route
so I would know precisely what your work was about.
And then I went to college. My bike just went so far.
A pretty wise investment was my fantastic car.
You said, "I looked it over. I like the way it drives."
But I knew I would buy it the moment you arrived.
My studies helped me DJ and kept me far from home.
But I had learned quite early to never feel alone.
Except while on my Honda, I leave it all behind.
And having Mom ride on it, I had to mastermind.

Now with little Kellie, more things are crystal clear.
By the way, I won't do drugs and haven't sipped a beer.
That may seem unimportant, but being 34
has opened for me journeys I never saw before.
I've still got lots of learning. You taught me never quit.
And being blessed with Kellie, I've got control of it.
And let me tell you something. Now that I'm a dad,
these last eight years with Kellie—the BEST I've ever had.
These are just a few things that prove you always cared.
And with your love and lessons, I'm never ever scared.

Gifted author? Phooey. I just sit down and write
about whatever strikes me or things I may dislike.
Yes, I must admit it. Sometimes I'm rather shocked
how easily the words flow in writings I concoct.
One day, me get published? I might. I write enough.
But with my baby daughter, free time's a little tough.
Just admit I'm human, and one day, I'll get tired;
or just retire early to keep from getting fired.
Personal reflections on quickly passing years
can bring a lot of laughter with some sporadic tears.
Let's just say I'm being the best dad I can be,
resourcing love and lessons you spent time teaching me.

Writing so much at one time or another, I was bound to probably lose a few that had meant lots to me. I may never somehow recollect all I have written or stumble upon all of my misplaced writings. To do so would be nothing short of a miracle. But this one was NOT in Kellie's Poetic Diary, and I am positive she is proud to have it here in her poetic biography.

DESTRUCTION IN DADE

I'm painting this dwelling for Felix and Pat.
Well, actually, I'm doing a lot more than that.
Hurricane Andrew tore through this whole town,
and left homes in shambles and flat on the ground.
The early news photos show Homestead is gone;
and not only houses, but also the lawns.
The awful destruction, most never have seen;
with winds gusting over 214.
Then Country Walk, albeit quiet and calm,
resembles a hit by a nuclear bomb.
The loss is enormous. With trees and roads clear,
we've resumed rebuilding and relieving fears.
Homebuilders are frantically trying to help,
while homeowners wander in spite of themselves.

But here at the Fanti's, the walls are intact;
while everything else—either broken or cracked.
It's not a good feeling to be in this place,
so that's why I brought a much happier face.
No it's not my face—I've got way too much stress.
What I brought with me likes to wear a nice dress.
Kellie is learning and since it's all new,
it helps peak her interest with plenty to do.
She's very well-mannered and brings me my tea,

and gives me more hints for her biography.
Yes, I keep writing. The muse is alive.
It doesn't keep hours from 7 to 5.
But really she's here for another intent.
When Pat read my poems with high compliments,
I promised I'd bring Kellie with me sometime.
While fixing this house, I write more of my rhymes.
It seems new additions are what most will get,
but here, a new roof keeps us from getting wet.
So while I'm surrounded by tears and despair,
my 3-foot tall angel sits right over there.

I got to meet Pat and her entire family during this horrible ordeal, and even went back numerous times to help with other projects once the home was fully restored. Pat was a gracious host and even though I got paid well for the work, it seemed less and less like a job as time went on. I was thrilled Kellie enjoyed going there so much, as I had a huge worklist. Kim even joined us at times. These were more situations where Kellie adapted well and was always willing to do what was necessary . . . all the while keeping that sweet, wonderful personality on display for everyone around to benefit from.

TRIP TO CA

We got there quite early; excited to be
the first time in CA since late '83.
Back then, I was star struck and stayed in L.A.,
but I brought my daughter for THIS special day.
No, just a second. Let me bite my lip.
It's more like a whole week we've planned on this trip.
A week of adventurous fun everyday
and Kellie's first time here. She may wanna' stay.
We flew to the northern part to see some sights
and visit some state parks for later at night.
Faye brought some scrapbooks of grandkids back home,
while I was there sharing a few of my poems.
We saw other cousins for family bonds,
but also had tickets to Olivia Newton-John.
We went through the hug line again in three rooms
so our prior plans, we now could resume.
We planned a whole week—with everyday full
of places to visit. I mean, that's no bull.
With Liv at the Fair, Monday at Six-Flags,
those in themselves were reasons to brag.
The concert was something. We sat really close.
And everyone gasped when, for just ME, she posed.
Kellie knew this night was special to me,
and photos we took turned out beautifully.
Creating a binder of poems for her,
I set it on her stage. The rest is a blur.
For the sheer reason that Kellie was here,
meant I got to show her all I held dear.

We drove down the coast all the way to L.A.,
and stopped at the sign saying "Hollywood—this way."
Mann's Chinese Theater and Walk of Fame stars:
we paused lots for pics and to watch the bizarres.
Kellie, near 13, was not ready for
what Hollywood offered: a bit too hardcore.
We slept late, ran errands, and relaxed one day.
That night, we ate at the Rainforest Cafe.
We packed up a cooler with food and some drinks,
but left out the oatmeal raisin cookies, I think.
With Mexico being so close to us now,
we drove to the border and then turned around.
At least she could say she saw Mexican lands,
as that was all we had time for in our plans.
Lunch in San Diego, was more for iced tea.
Although Kellie liked it, it was mainly for me.
We had to drive back up the coast for our flight,
and Kellie was tired so she slept through the night.
As with all vacations, our time went too fast;
but mem'ries with Kellie will forever last.

After having such a great time in the early 80's visiting California, I was eager to share it with my daughter. Kellie and I finally made it out there in 1999 and went from the northern area all the way down past San Diego to Mexico. It was a sightseeing adventure, but I had planned numerous events along the way and it was one of my most enjoyable times with her. A published poem never fades.

Holiday Cheer

SHRIEK-A-BOO

Kellie said "Throw me a party."
I said "OK. Now where and when?"
She said " . . . a Halloween party.
Thanksgiving's next month. Before then.
I want a really fun party,
one they'll remember for years."
Peaking my imagination,
I knew it must include some fears.
I asked her to be more specific.
"We have to work out some details."
After brainstorming for hours,
our list did include some entrails.
Themed food was Gummy Bear Ghoulies,
and peeled grapes would pass for eyeballs.
Twizzlers makes good creepy crawlers:
some leggy, while others were small.
Apples in caramel were normal.
To make sure we made the guests squirm,
brains would be kale leaves in Jello;
and slimy spaghetti for worms.
We had fun naming the menu
and other foods that made her laugh.
CD's and records to die for—

I said I'd bring a phonograph.
She put a guest list together,
while I went to work on a box.
See, I was building a coffin
and other things for chains and locks.
Making the coffin was simple:
a long crate with room on the sides.
Kellie was in on the secret
and swore to keep mum the surprise.
With guests, the top wouldn't open.
To make sure, I screwed down the top.
And I'd lie still while inside it.
In time, the front panel would drop.
The themed decorations were flawless.
Her guests all showed up and on time.
Once they had tested the coffin,
I knew these fooled kids were all mine.
After all, what kind of parent
would willingly lie in a box
during a Halloween party?
That's certainly unorthodox.
After about 40 minutes,
and all Kellie's friends had no clue,
"Dracula" rolled from that coffin;
and frightened those kids with a BOO!!!

Needless to say, kids were jumping
like Pringles chips popping their lids.
"Dracula" ran through the party
and scared the wits out of those kids.
Dressed in my Dracula costume,
and Kellie played it to a T;
she acted scared like the others,
and never told them it was me.
Kellie said even weeks later,
she still was the topic of choice.
Others wished they'd been invited,
like girls and a few older boys.
Now, Kellie's not so poetic;
and since I kept still in a crate,
no rhymes are left for this poem.
Trust us; the party was great.

This was one truly remarkable party. I was able to spend time with Kellie in all the planning and and as she saw the coffin being made, she was excited to know her friends were never going to forget being scared. This poem is just about as vivid as HD video.

HOLIDAY SLUSH

Spending time shopping through windows,
or dodging down a crowded aisle,
doesn't keep my boat a floatin'
and nothing to keep me in style.
Kellie finds all sorts of reasons
to put off what I say we do.
The truth is, and she's unaware,
I still get it done when we're through.
One reason is when I'm with her,
our time is casual and free.
Everything's done when I get her,
so it's always just her and me.
We get exercise down the aisles
and chat about things we don't want.
However, she might get lucky
and find a new dress she can flaunt.
Stores always open long hours
to handle the holiday rush.
Kellie would rather have bon-bons,
or slurp on a raspberry slush.
Santa can bring us our presents.
He's got elves to wrap and to tape.
Halloween's much more exciting

when we put on masks and our capes.
But since the tree's up and the ocean
is too cold to swim in this year,
we might as well check out some bargains
and welcome this holiday cheer.
So bring on the mad rush. We're ready,
'cause nothing will catch us off guard.
Kellie has slushies to cool her,
and I've got my gold credit card.

Where many dread the holiday rushes and get very frustrated, Christmas was a joyous time for Kellie and me because it was always casual. We got together and just enjoyed each other's company . . . and that is what our Christmas spirit was all about . . . not gifts and greed.

SANTA SAYS . . .

Christmas is over . . . I'm sorry 'bout that.
I needed to alter my red suit and hat.
You see, Mrs. Kringle is sick with the flu,
as are my best elves. So what could I do?
Helpers were lifting some bags on my sleigh,
and slipped on some toys that weren't put away.
Three of my reindeer aren't feeling their best.
The doctor came by and he prescribed rest.
My belly is jelly. I still Ho Ho Ho,
but Rudolph was sneezing and stuffed up his glow.
Thank goodness for Donner. He's good over land,
but struggled through storms in Spain and Japan.
Forgive me for running a little behind.
I promise next Christmas, I'll be here on time.

Again, another spur of the moment poem that came out of being late with the personal gift-giving due to trying to finish jobs for clients before the holidays began. Funny thing is, these can be added to so easily.

A MOM FOR CHRISTMAS

The 14 small children I'd laughed with so far,
had started to become a little bizarre.
They all wanted gadgets and big-screen TV's.
I chuckled a few words and gave them a squeeze.
I happened to notice, while taking a break,
the ice storm outside had turned into snowflakes.
And yes, I'd decided, this year, after all,
I'd play Santa Claus at the Coral Square Mall.
I had on my suit and my beard and white hair,
but when she walked up to me, I had to stare.
This blond little girl came and sat on my knee.
I asked her, "What would you like under your tree?"
That's when I stopped as she lowered her head.
After a moment, these sad words she said:
    "Santa, I'm sorry that my clothes are torn.
    I'm sorry the soles of my shoes are all worn.
    But I lost my mommy the day I was born,
    and Daddy was never the same.
    I guess that he loved me but in recent years,
    I've been feeling lonely with sadness and tears.
    He never abused me. Even with all the beers,
    I never felt he was to blame.

It's now been two years since he died in his car.
I live with my grandma who doesn't live far.
I even tried wishing on a shiny star,
but maybe that's too high to aim.
Santa, you bring gifts to kids when they're good.
And I've tried all year to be the best that I could.
If there's any possible way at all, would
you, Santa, please bring me a mom?"
I couldn't believe it. Chills ran down my spine.
It made me reflect on that mother of mine.
She never had left me. I'd felt so secure,
but this girl was hurting. Of that, I was sure.
My wife of six years was there playing my elf
and heard the girl's words and lost it herself.
Here I was, Santa, all jolly with joy.
This poor girl was not here to ask for a toy.
My voice cracked. I stuttered a gentle reply,
but to no avail. She started to cry.
I felt so unworthy, so helpless, and yet,
I vowed to myself somehow I would get
a nice home and mother for this little girl.
Could it be that hard? I had a whole world
from which to choose one. So later that night,
I spoke to my wife and she said alright.

What seemed like forever has now come to pass.
We spent a year bonding and then she smiled as
we said "Live with us. You'll have your own room."
I made her this promise without my costume.
"I'm not God nor Santa. I can't disappear.
I'll give you my best every day of the year.
Just know that we love you. If you're ever sad,
she's 'Mommy' and I'm your new dad."

Numerous times, I dressed as Santa for Kellie before she was a
teen and she considered herself very fortunate. One of our favorite TV
movies was "A Mom for Christmas" starring Olivia. So it inspired me
to merge the two and write a poem where the little girl is less fortunate
and has no parents. This was a tearjerker for Kellie.

CHRISTMAS IN FLORIDA

A Florida Christmas is all kinds of fun.
We rollerblade, play, and swim in the sun.
We're not into snowmen nor stoking hot fires.
We skip down the street and hear caroling choirs.
Now don't get me wrong. I'm not very old,
but I'll keep the sun and you keep your cold.

Your winters are frigid. Our winters are hot.
You shovel off driveways while we swim a lot.
To all of your family from all of us here,
we wish you glad tidings for a wonderful year.

These are more of the short poems that we would hang on holiday gifts. I never knew how much "in the holiday spirit" I would be, but if I was with Kellie, the muse normally followed. I just had to listen.

PRE-GIFTS

Christmas is coming, but we have no snow.
The temp, I believe, is 60 or so.
The presents are wrapped and under the tree,
but those Kellie's hidden from her mom and me.
We hope that your season is filled with good cheer.
Have a wonderful holiday from all of us here.

Mrs. Claus likes to knit and so you wouldn't cry,
she made you a towel to keep you nice and dry.

You don't need a blanket. You got one already.
And you're much too old for a train set or teddy.
You can build snowmen to your heart's content,
and come March or April, you'll ask where they went.
But here in the sunshine, the ocean's our pond.
We'll swim while you shiver, too cold to respond.
You'll miss all the wisdom we often impart.
Instead, we sent presents straight from our hearts.

Christmas is coming without any snow.
Sunny with blue skies and 60 or so.
The gifts are still wrapped and under the tree,
but those Kellie's hidden from her mom and me.
We hope that your season is filled with good cheer.
To all, Merry Christmas and a Happy New Year.

I called these little poems this because we would come up with little quips to attach to a wrapped present, and we felt it was better than just a tag or a sticker. Usually, we tied them to gifts we were sending to family out-of-state. However, if the spirit was high and the muse was close by, little quips might turn into nice-sized poems quite rapidly. And then they might get sent, but not saved.

SIGNS OF CHRISTMAS

You're turning four, but the holiday's here:
referring to Christmas, not the New Year.
You were outside giving bread to the ducks.
Santa came by in his fiery red truck.
Remote-control cars have to roll off the road
while we finish groceries. We got a carload.
Florida sunshine means we'll have no snow.
You don't seem to mind it the older you grow.
Presents surrounding a brightly-lit tree:
wond'ring if they are for you or for me.
Assorted paper and size give no clues.
Lacking a tag means how are we to choose?
You can sneak over to grab one and shake.
Better be careful. One could be a snake.
Maybe you'll pick one: the first one you see,
and just rip it open. Rest it on your knee.
It's funny. To you, it means taking each flap
and tearing through gently, or something like that.
I'm laughing. I know that you'll choose to, one day,
keep the box and throw the present away.

THE HOLIDAY BLUES

We found out you're sick and that's sad to hear,
'cause Christmas just passed and it's a new year.
It's a celebration with loved ones and friends,
but when one is illin', the happiness ends.
We'll do what we can to help cheer you up,
but as bad as you feel, we'll need more than luck.
We could feed you hot soup and tuck you in bed,
while wave pools or baby dolls dance in your head.
Or say a quiet prayer for God's miracle touch
to get you well soon 'cause we love you so much.
And leave a few gifts . . . but wait! 'Cause you're sick,
your sniffle is germs. Let's get out of here quick!

On one of Kellie's rare holidays when she got sick, this was another poem that practically wrote itself. It was not an instant healing, but she did laugh when I shared this with her.

Gone,

But

Not

Forgotten

WHY GOD?

"Why hast Thou forsaken me?"
You've heard that many times.
Your only Son cried out that phrase
with Calvary's hill to climb.
You took Your loving hand away
and let Him die alone.
And now You've done the same again
long distance from your throne.
She was so young, so full of life,
and doing all she could;
taking care of her son, too.
I always knew she would.
But God, You'd given her to me,
the brightest light I'd known.
So why'd You take her suddenly
and call my daughter home?
Did the angels up above
have better things to do?
Was she needed all that bad?
What was it God, for You?
You have the power to create
and still You let things die.
You took my Kellie way too soon.
Please God, tell me why.

"Why hast Thou forsaken me?"
My heart cries out to you
to help me understand your plan
and what I'm meant to do.
My source of purpose died Monday.
I haven't stopped the fall.
Oh God, You took MY angel home
when Kellie left us all.

This was only the first of many that poured from my soul when I lost my daughter. A few days later, when I spoke to the pastor who was going to perform the service, he asked me if I was going to have a few words to say. I honestly told him it would be impossible for me to maintain my composure, but that I had written a poem; although I was sure he would not want to share it. Surprisingly, the name of his service was "God, Why?" and he recited this word for word. This poem serves as a vivid and heartfelt reminder of that service and all the turmoil I was feeling when I tearfully wrote it.

KELLIE (GOD TOOK YOU AWAY)

To see your lovely face again
would be a dream come true . . .
To hold you in my arms again
just like I used to do . . .
To hear your laughter, see your smile
on each and ev'ry day . . .
But those are only in my mind
since God took you away.
He took you up to be with Him
and filled my eyes with tears.
It seems He turned His back on me
and cursed my final years.
He took away your chance to be
a mother and a wife,
and left me down here all alone
in this depressing life.
Kellie, you were all I wanted,
all I ever had.
Yet, I'm told to lift my head
and somehow not be sad.
When I finally get up there,
I'll lift my head up high;
and with my anger now unleashed,
fight why you had to die.

THE NUTSHELL

I put the box of toys away
I'd brought down from the shelf.
I sorted all the photographs
of you with no one else.
It took me many hours as
I worked through all the tears,
and wondered how a nutshell could
surround so many years.
"To put it in a nutshell" was
supposed to be a way
where I'd explain so clearly
Kellie's tragic holiday.
Every time a friend called wanting
details with the news,
it was ripping through my soul.
My mind was still confused.
Recalling detailed memories
blurred by the death of you:
to put them in a nutshell was
the hardest thing to do.
Explaining all the details still
torments my aching heart

and how that fateful morning just
keeps tearing me apart.
I would have been there for you
if you'd just called out my name,
but God had other plans and now
my life's forever changed.
I have to let you go, dear.
I need to find a way.
But still I'm crying, honey,
each night and every day.

Still a constant struggle and well-meaning friends and family just have to understand this is not something you turn off in public. I don't wish it on anyone, but until you walk in another's shoes, you have no clue at all what it is like to lose one so dearly loved.

HOW???

How can you call me a father
when Kellie, my daughter, is gone?
How can there be celebration
when Almighty God claimed his own?
How can I look in the mirror
without somehow seeing her eyes?
It's why I sit here now in anguish
and even God turns from my cries.
Our videos show me her feelings
with pictures that never will fade.
I now watch her singing and dancing;
the sweet, goofy faces she made.
I strain to absorb all her laughing,
but drown out her laughter with tears.
My God, she was so sweet and pretty
and got even better each year.

She loved her koala named One B,
and cherished it near her whole life.
Until recently, she misplaced him.
It cut through that girl like a knife.
I'd shared verses with her about him;
some written like he'd said the words.
How he missed her playing with "Cookie"

made her laughter the sweetest I'd heard.
I'd always thought koalas were cuties,
although I grew up on a farm.
But loved she shared my admiration.
All four-legged creatures have charm.
There's so many stories about him.
She took him almost everywhere;
then hated the day that she lost him.
I'll always remember that bear.

I took her on trips for vacations.
Our favorite was at Blizzard Beach;
that huge waterpark there at Disney.
It never seemed far out of reach.
To spend the whole day there was awesome.
When older, she took it in stride;
but made sure we did Summit Plummet—
their 5-story drop waterslide.
I'll never forget going to Naples
and getting up just before dawn.
We'd already done all the packing;
grabbed cooler and towels and were gone.
She kept counting gators while singing.
I had no idea what we'd do.
I just knew the fun day before us
would be filled with laughter and new.

We'd packed up food for barbecuing
and brought a big raft and some rope.
We got a choice table there early.
For breakfast, we shared cantaloupe.
The ocean was warm and inviting.
She jumped in and let out a yell.
I set up the chairs and umbrella
and held down Mom's blanket with shells.
I then put some air in the mattress
and tied the long rope at the end.
The waves were not big but were perfect.
She'd get a good ride with the wind.
What shocked me were all the onlookers.
Her riding the waves made a crowd
gather up close to the shoreline.
I saw in her eyes she was proud.
It's like kids looked up at their parents
and wondered why they hadn't brought
a raft of some kind they could ride on.
Next time, they might give it some thought.
Her riding was, like, never-ending.
I pulled her back after each wave.
A few of them broke a bit early,
but she held on tight and was brave.

I liked, that with me, she was active.
We spent lots of time at the parks:
on swingsets when she was a toddler;
when older, we'd skate well past dark.
We also rode bikes on the pathways,
especially at Miami Beach,
while spending the nights at the Campbell's.
She made it quite easy to teach.
She took a bad spill there while skating
and tried to go through some wet sand.
She scratched up her leg rather badly,
along with her face and her hand.
She cried as I pulled up behind her.
I picked her up off of the trail,
and after some gauze and some cleansing,
she said she'd wear a ponytail.
We used lots of film at the Campbell's.
She painted and built her first tent.
And then she got older and wiser.
I wondered where all those years went.

I always enjoyed my daughter,
no matter what we chose to do.
It always was fun and exciting,
and each time was like something new.

But finding the owls: that was precious.
We found their small nest in the dirt,
and felt they might need some protection.
We used some sticks and my t-shirt.
Her eyes gleamed when just a week later,
we saw they had put up a fence;
allowing us to keep observing,
while they had a bit more defense.

And, oh yes, my one cat was Tiger.
I had him while just a young boy.
Then Kellie's first also was Tiger.
I smiled with a soul-touching joy.
She'd chosen him without my knowledge.
From him, I knew she'd never part.
She had quite a love for all creatures.
That part of her melted my heart.

So yes, all the pictures and poems
that reflect on all that we shared
lend credence to all our endeavors
and just how much both of us cared.
My one shot at being a father:
it lasted just 24 years.
Yet none of the musing has gotten
me past all the heartache and tears.

Sometimes folks have preparations.
They know what will happen and when.
But when it's a sudden occurrence,
there's no preparation, my friend.
It feels like a freight train ran through me;
and took with it all I was worth.
I never, for even a moment,
thought I'd lose what I helped to birth.
Just sore, tear-filled eyes and heartsickness
are feelings I know all too well.
My one chance to be a good father . . .
has ended. I'm going through hell!

This was written partially on one Father's Day and then revised and added to the following year. I must say it is no fun being in this mindset. It is a mind-numbing experience, yet with persistent pain. I am not sure what the benefit is supposed to be for writing these, but perhaps they are for someone else's benefit. I certainly hope so.

ANGELS ON YOUR PILLOW

The light's gone out inside of me.
It's hard to tell you why.
I used to be so strong and sure
and found no need to cry.
I used to take on anything.
It mattered not the size.
I often felt that I could bring
a few words to the wise.
And with convictions, stronger still,
enforcing moral code,
I strived to show the best of me
whatever seeds I sowed.
Memorial Day changed all that when
my daughter passed away.
Talk about a shock and awe
and unforgiving day.

I can't begin to understand
nor why you had to go.
You'd meant so much to me down here.
And watching Tyler grow
was gonna' be another way
you got to shine your light;

by mothering him, with peace and love,
and bedtime books at night.

I stand here at your gravesite now.
My face is red with tears.
My mind keeps flashing through your life
of just 24 years.
Of seven billion people here,
God wanted only you.
He'd filled your heart and soul with love.
You were an angel, too.
What was His plan? His reasoning
to take you suddenly?
He surely had to realize
what this would do to me.
I guess He felt I'd had enough
to somehow get me through,
but children aren't supposed to die
before their parents do.
I'd imagined many times
us standing at Death's door.
But it was me then passing through.
You still had life, and more.
It seemed the possibility
would only be in stunts.

To have you go before your time—
I never thought it once.
And yet, you're up in Heaven now
and I'm down here alone.
You've been embraced by angels
and you've seen God on His throne.
I see you're held by loving angels.
No more need to weep.
The angels on your pillow dance
before you go to sleep.

Talking to a good friend prior to writing this, she was telling me about how she had missed her father when he passed away. In her description of what her father had told her after passing, she used the phrase "angels on your pillow." I stopped her immediately and told her that would be the title of my next poem. I had no idea why, but my muse had spoken. A few days later, at Kellie's gravesite, my conversation with Kellie included her saying the same exact phrase when she described angels that dance on her pillow. The above poem immediately began to fill my head, and driving home through tear-filled eyes, these words just poured out of me. Eerie, but true.

"DADDY, GOD IS CALLING!"

I just came by your grave site and I found you waiting there.
You still were in your T-shirt and your jeans and blowing hair.
I thought I'd say a few words that were heavy on my mind,
but it was good to see you since I miss you all the time.
We hugged for like an hour and cried. You finally let me go,
and then expressed ideas that you had wanted me to know.

"Daddy, I'm in Heaven because
there, I couldn't stay.
You gave me all the love you had
and it grew everyday.
I know you're contemplating
a somewhat final deal.
Come on, you know better.
It's not the way to feel.
Daddy, please don't rush it.
You know I had to go.
And I know what you're thinking . . .
but it's no way to show
the people that still love you:
well, it would break their hearts
if you were just to leave them
with no clues where to start.
I know it came so sudden
my coming up here now,
but I was down there hurting;
in pain. But anyhow,
you have much more to do now,

and then I'm sure you'll see
that it is as was written
for you as well as me.
I was your little pumpkin;
the apple of your eye.
You cherished me my whole life,
so there's no need to cry.
Daddy, I'm so sorry
and I know it hurts you bad.
You would've tried to change things
with the money that you had.
You feel you had the power
to do all that and more.
But Daddy, God has plans for you
and someone you'll adore."

Kellie, I can't take it 'cause you were my everything.
We may have joked about it, but you really made me sing.
I had no time of warnings and no chances to prepare
that He'd allow confusion here, and then take you up there.
Then you said,

"Most of all, you know
I've always loved you, Dad.
I could have listened more
to make the most of what we had.
But I was wrapped up in my own life,
struggling all the while;
but knew deep in my heart,
I always could count on your smile.

Please watch over Tyler,
and guide him everyday.
Tell him that I love him so,
although I went away.
Share with him our moments.
Help him feel the love
and goodness that we always felt.
I'll watch from here above.
Share with him your writings
and he will come to see
his heart will fill with goodness;
the same you had for me.
Share with him your wisdom
of what is right and wrong.
Let him know you'll always love him
for however long.
Dad, you know I loved him.
My son meant everything.
He put a song deep in my heart
although I couldn't sing.
But Daddy, I'm not sad here.
I know that may sound weird.
But I can see all you guys
and it's not like I had feared.
The hurt and pain and anger
have all been washed away.
And hey! I'm 10 pounds lighter.
I lost it in one day.
You have me in your dreams now.
I fill your thoughts and mind.

And I need you to listen now.
You need to be less kind.
Many friends keep asking you,
'What happened?' 'Where?' and 'Why?'
If only they could understand
how all those make you cry.
You're on a rollercoaster,
much too fast for you to take.
You're helping other people,
yet continuing to ache.
Your heart and soul need mending.
Please just focus on you now.
And since I'm still your angel,
I can make this solemn vow.
Remember what God promised.
Just live your life for good,
so God will give more blessings
than you ever thought He would.
Your mom is up here also.
She welcomed me in first.
We want to see you live your dreams
and let that bubble burst.
And, oh, remember fishing?
We talked about that, too.
I was only four then,
but she was so proud of you.
Daddy, God is calling us.
We don't want Him to wait.
I promise we'll watch over you
and your life will be great.

**But this is most important,
and don't you dare forget.
God has a plan for all our lives . . .
and you ain't lived yours yet."**

This was another of our "gravesite chats" where the words and flow overwhelmed me. Out-of-body experience, no, but the conversation went as it is written here. I'm not sure why some come so easily. I never went to the cemetery expecting anything, never more than a cold reminder of the most wonderful person I'd ever known.

MISSING HER

I'm missing all my daughter's sounds,
no matter when nor where.
I'm missing how she greeted me
with ever-changing hair.
I'm missing all she told me and
what mattered to her most.
I'm missing all the times we swam
both here and the West Coast.
I'm missing how we made up games
and played them many times.
I'm missing how I heard her laugh-
ter with my silly rhymes.
I miss how Kellie looked at me
with true love and respect,
and growing closer everyday;
thrilled each time that we met.
I miss the color of those eyes;
the same green tint as mine.
I shared with her so many things,
and thought we had more time.
But then it all came to an end.
She left so suddenly.

She left me here so lonely now,
forever I will be.
It's not supposed to be this way.
I'm not supposed to cry.
I'm not supposed to see my daughter
pass before I die.
I'm not supposed to feel my heart
ripped wildly from my chest,
or hear from family and friends
it's all some stupid test.

How can it be a God that loves
allows us so much pain?
How can it be we're made to suffer
time and time again?
It doesn't seem to matter, God.
I tried to figure out
Your reasoning to take her still.
What was that all about?
I cry my heart out, night and day.
You took her just past dawn.
Without a word of warning, God,
my baby girl was gone.
To lay it all before me, it
just makes no sense at all.

And that's why I'm still heartsick
here, continuing to fall.

The anguish is so overwhelming. To lose a child with no warning, out of sheer nonsense, and have no closure is to find oneself spinning in the middle of a square room with no corners; where painful torture is the only thing listed on the daily activities.

I'LL NEVER LEAVE YOU

I could search the cosmos, but I'll never ever know
how God showed a blessing by commanding you to go.
Gone, but not forgotten, Kellie, you are this to me;
while I'm stuck here crying, bathing in my misery.

**Dad, I see you crying
and I'm sorry that I'm gone.
I see your heart's in turmoil
every night through well past dawn.
You're hardly ever sleeping
in the midst of all your tears,
because I came to Heaven
after just a few short years.
Dad, you always told me that
you'd never leave my side,
and yes, I always felt it
in the love you'd never hide.
The things you taught me, Daddy,
that I failed to sometimes show,
have brought to me much comfort
and in ways you'll never know.
I knew that as a youngster,
I could never let you down.
You taught me about pride, like**

every time I won a crown.
I loved to be a princess.
Dressing up was so much fun.
Some trophies may say different,
but I felt like number one.
You praised me on my poise.
I was the apple of your eye.
You shared with me your poems,
and you know they made me cry.
I didn't understand it.
All I knew was you would smile
in spite of some disaster
we would fix after awhile.
You took me on vacations;
more fun than I ever dreamed.
I shared your love for thrill rides:
rarely scared, but always screamed.
You had a way about you,
and at times, with so much ease.
I'd tell you what I needed
and you never failed to please.
And sometimes I was stubborn.
I am well aware of that;
but you let it wash away
like at a laundromat.

Now, that all seems so long ago.
My time on Earth is done.
But God has granted me this time
for talking one-on-one.
When we went out to Tampa
and, all day, I rode the float,
while you stood in the ocean.
Well, I made a mental note
and thanked you 12 years later
in a very special way;
by showing up with Tyler
for the cruise on Father's Day.
Your mind was so creative,
which you taught me how to be,
but I worked harder at it
'cause you had way more than me.
Although you never thought it
'cause with you, I did no wrong.
It's what you always told me
in your poetry and songs.
I knew I had a daddy
that would love me without fail;
who made the yellow scrapbook,
then wrote Tania and the whale.
The special bond between us,

I then fully understood
when God blessed me with Tyler;
so much better than just good.
I felt the same way you had
all those many years ago;
and vowed to show the same love
while we all would watch him grow.
Dad, God blessed me with Tyler,
just like He blessed you with me.
We never know for how long . . .
just the way it has to be.
I fly with wings of angels,
so Dad please, don't sit and cry.
I'll live like this in Heaven,
so Dad, see, I didn't die.
Oh Dad, you never left me
and it's all that I can do
to now return the favor
and vow never to leave you.

Another "gravesite chat" that overwhelmed me. I didn't say much, but she had me in tears the entire time . . .

MY KELLIE

To contemplate the way you died
and how you must have felt;
I still can't even go there yet.
I'm just beside myself.
To be so torn by all the facts
and mysteries in the dark,
it's gone way past confusing,
with an indelible mark.
And no one has an answer.
God Himself is keeping mum.
I could walk through briars
and I'd still feel less than numb.

I wish I was your superman
so I could fly away,
and come to break down Heaven's door
and bring you back today.
I don't know when. I don't know why
God writes the scripts He does.
And then He claims we have free will.
Well, maybe it's because
He knew that He'd be lonely then.
And with His plans for me,

He wanted you next to Him and
watch from His balcony.
But Kellie, we had no goodbyes.
And Tyler misses you.
It's just a lousy thing He pulled
that's left me black-and blue.
So I've not been much of a show
with all that's got me down.
He should have left you here with me
and saved your halo crown.

A very difficult poem to write with all the visuals . . . I actually grieve
for any and every parent who has lost a child they loved. The situation
is handled so many ways, yet nothing seems to calm the troubled mind.

IF I WERE A GOD

(to the tune of Beyonce's "If I Were a Boy")

If I were a god
I would need just a day
I'd tell all my angels to pick out
a tortured soul on Earth and to pray

I'd march into Hell
and slap Satan around
Multiply his pain for tormenting
my children here on Earth, and prove
I'm the god still wearing the crown

If I were a god
I'm sure I would understand
how it feels to lose a loved one
and comfort both the woman and man
I'd listen to them
'cause I know how it hurts
when you lose the one I gave you
and don't think you should have to
when much of what I had got destroyed

If I were a god
I would calm many storms
Let me use my wrath where needed
To punish evil would be the norm

But God, You put Yourself first
and change the rules as You go
when You know that I've been faithful
so just wait for me to come home . . . I'll come home

If I were a god
I'm sure I would understand
to not take a loved one quickly
nor needlessly hurt a worthy man
I'd listen to him
'cause I know how it hurts
when you lose the one I gave you
and don't know why you have to
when much of what I had got destroyed

It's a little too late for you to give back
Say it's just a mistake . . . I won't forgive you for that
You thought I'd accept it all?
You thought wrong
But you're just a god

Seems you don't understand
No you don't understand
just how much I loved my daughter
You know I was a worthy man

You didn't listen to her
You never cared how it hurt
when she loved the son you gave her
and longed to be a mother
then everything we had got destroyed
But you're just a god

I really enjoyed the original version performed by Beyonce and continued to play it from her CD. But the more I listened to it, the more it struck a nerve with Kellie's recent passing, and soon, I was rewriting the lyrics in my head. After a week of trying to relax and get away from everything, (which didn't work), the new lyrics were all I could think of. And driving home from my week long getaway, I was in tears because I could not get the song out of my head. And then, after 2 ½ days of no sleep, to keep a promise to a friend, I recorded myself singing it and posted it on YouTube.

BIRTH DAY

How could I, without warning,
have known that you'd be gone
to Heaven on your birthday,
with angels, singing songs?
Why would I ever think that
my years of having you
would so abruptly end be-
fore turning 52?
We never got the pleasure
to share so many things
like trying on long dresses
or checking diamond rings.
'Cause all these things, a father
is looking forward to.
To see just how my teachings
of love affected you.
True, your childish actions
had made me laugh a lot.
And we had bonded closely,
with poetry snapshots.
We said we're getting closer
and healing some old scars.
But God, He took you from me

to live among the stars.
I guess your pain is over
and joy is all you know,
but still I'm left here crying,
the lowest of all lows.
To celebrate a birthday,
makes sense while still alive,
but with your unknown causes,
you couldn't then survive.
I guess I should be happy
you passed through Heaven's door,
but there's no celebration
in my heart anymore.

Her birthday became all about her birth day in this one and how only a little time had passed before it was all over. Slight difference, maybe, but to a mournful father, there was no cause for celebrations that day. These might be difficult to read one page after the other, but I would still rather be in the readers' shoes than in this author's.

YOUR PLEASANT STREAM

I am here, your pleasant stream,
flowing through your soul.
Stitching up your broken heart
and helping you feel whole.
Easing all your aches and pains
and smiling down on you.
Sharing all God's promises
of what He says He'll do.
When your head is hurting
and your eyes are feeling blurred,
I'll wrap you in my loving arms
and soothe you with my words.
So for now, relax your mind
and melt right into me.
Doctors, they may charge you,
but my services are free.

We all suffer through trial periods of our lives. Perhaps it is because we are dishonest with others or ourselves, or we waste time regretting a past mistake. "Cary" actually means "pleasant stream" and Kellie knew she had a sensitive father who cared about her no matter what and always was willing to do whatever was needed.

THEY SAY

They say I should be happy.
But why? Are you still here?
They say I should sing praises.
But why? Who's gonna' hear?
They know I lost my daughter,
but still insist that I
somehow put it behind me
and dry my tear-filled eyes.
I can't begin to fathom
just why they say these things,
when I've repeated truly
you were my everything.
Is it just in their nature
to be this cruel and cold?
Has their heart never opened
when things can't be controlled?
I can't sit here and ponder
the things they say and do.
I won't sit here in judgement
with all they've put me through.
I'll let them finish talking
since I can't leave this place.
They better finish quickly
and get out of my face.

GOD, OUR SPIRITS LIKE TO SING

God, You don't amaze me with good works anymore.
This world is full of crazies and Satan's keeping score.
He's batting near .900 and stealing all the souls
of children You were loving. And You call this control?
Satan's down here ruling and laughing in Your face,
while we, as humble servants, are struggling for Your grace.
You made it rain forever with Noah and the flood;
demanding sacrifices with offerings and blood.
Where's the wrathful vengeance You used those years ago?
The Bible says You promise to help us fight these foes.
Well, Satan has us cornered while yelling in our ears.
Your still, small voice won't cut it to overcome these fears.
He's got his demon angels, that You once called Your own,
to terrorize Your children, while You sit on Your throne.
He knows! He's read the Bible. He's got a starring role.
It's not the war he's after, but just another soul.

You've thrown us in a battle that few of us will win,
and this is all because of our aptitude to sin?
We never ate the apple. Eve did, in paradise.
Her family then suffered. They paid their hefty price.
Fast forward to the present. So where's our guiding light?
You send us in stripped naked, expecting us to fight.
Religious leaders shout out "God reigns! We'll win the war!"
It seems to me they're clueless to what this fight is for.
They use their books and timelines, yet what I know, I found.
The battle's raging onward. They're sitting out the round.

They muddle through translations. I read them all as one.
You were so great and vengeful, and then You sent Your Son
to show us being peaceful is such a moral trait.
But still, the fight is in us and that will make us great.
You strengthened mighty Samson. King David loved You so.
And even though they failed You, they both returned to show
that evil could be punished. And then the common man
would share Your love with others and help them understand.

It's just how we're created. You knew we'd be like this.
We can't become complacent and live with hit-or-miss.
We need to live with kindness; in peace and harmony?
Ok, that works for angels. That's how they're meant to be.
With numerous temptations, Christ never flinched a bit.
His life, for true salvation, was pure. He couldn't quit.
I still find fascinating His human frailties
and praying in the garden, "Remove this cup from me . . ."
His heart was bathed in kindness. Divine love filled His soul.
But He was on a mission and had to fill the role.
You showed us all Your mercy and sacrificed Your Son.
He had to hang there bleeding. Redemption had begun.
So He allowed transgressions to pierce His beating heart.
The Trinity idea? That's where this falls apart.
'Cause if You sent a Saviour—an angel dressed in skin,
then there's no crucifixion; no pain in a sure win.
Christ cried out You had left Him in all His agony.
It wasn't You, but Jesus who died on Calvary.
Your Son was seeking comfort while You sat on Your throne.
For death to overtake Him, You let Him hang alone.
He was a perfect human equipped with all the tools
to preach of life eternal when following Your rules.

Again, You made us different: have doubts, but fight despair.
The worst roads that we travel: You say You're waiting there.
Well, Satan keeps his demons along those bumpy roads,
and they can look like angels and lift our heavy loads.
And then before we know it, the path is dark and rough.
And then we feel surrounded, and faith seems not enough.
We cry out for assistance. Our weariness is great.
But then for many of us, the helping hand's too late.
It's almost like betrayal. We may have slipped a bit,
but You're our loving Father and it feels like You quit.
Refuse to help the weary, and they will come to see
when You take all You gave them, they'll feel similar to me.
For us, to lose a loved one, is just the same as death.
It makes us want to give up and breathe our final breath.
Surprisingly, You gave me a love I'd never known.
It was my daughter, Kellie, and through her, You have shown
You call us when we're needed and once we have confessed.
But You will only call us when worthy for our test.

And yet, in just mere moments, while feeling still betrayed,
I'm here for nothing more than a quiet accolade.
Make me your mighty servant. You've taken all I had.
You claim Almighty Father while I was just a dad.
I'm crying out and pleading for just a fighting chance
to quiet evildoers and bring back some romance.
'Cause Satan's drugs are worthless. I never drank his booze.
Let him send all his demons. My soul You'll never lose.
But if, for unknown reasons, You've got another plan,
then guide me to that playbook while I'm still just a man.
And let determination stitch up my fractured heart.

Direct my focus elsewhere to give me a fresh start.
I'll finish like a hero and then pass through Death's door;
and once I'm up in Heaven, I'll gladly fight some more.

Make me Your mighty angel, with angels at my side.
And then send us to Satan. We'll spank his blistered hide.
And two-thirds of Your angels, that he took down with him,
will have the Lake of Fire for their everlasting swim.
Divine justification will put those demons down.
We'll end this holy battle and polish up Your crown.
We'll gladly show that devil he wasted all his time,
and vanquish him in parsley, rosemary, sage, and thyme.
The torment will be over. Mankind will get to show
we did learn love from Jesus and how to make it grow.
Then show me to my mansion and let my daughter see
the richness there in Heaven You promised it would be.
The paths of our ancestors have proven just one thing.
While living in weak bodies, our spirits like to sing.

Controversial? As with any written work, you often need to read the
entire piece to grasp its potential and intended meanings. This insightful
and thought-provoking poem is no exception to that.

NOTHING LEFT TO SAY

Gloomy skies and tear-filled eyes
are how you greet each day.
'Cause when you've lost the one you love,
there's nothing left to say.
The aching head that throbs each day,
no pills can ever cure.
The loneliness of unshared thoughts,
of this, you know for sure.
To play around with someone's life
is not a way to be.
But people do it everyday
and maybe it's to see
just how much crap someone can take
before they lose their way.
They justify it foolishly.
There's nothing left to say.
Your lifelong friends may claim they care,
but come on, let's be real.
They're way too wrapped up in their lives
to take the time to feel
that deep inside your stricken heart,
you're fading fast away.
The fuse is lit and burning

in depressing, final days.
You try to take a stab at God
to feed your weary soul,
but yet, it seems He's turned His back
and you lose all control.
You struggle with and muddle through
to prove your worth, but then
your heart is crushed and spirit's broken,
time and time again.
Your fate is sealed. There's no time left
and nothing you can do.
Exhausted possibilities
are all that's left for you.
A hidden corner or some rat-
infested alley way
is where they find your rotting corpse.
There's nothing left to say.

We never know how a certain individual is going to react to heartache and tragic loss. We can make excuses for ourselves by just telling them to be stronger or we can justify less involvement while we deal with our own issues. All too often, we choose only one or the other, while a person in need drifts into depression and death.

ANOTHER HOLIDAY SPENT WITHOUT YOU

I spent another holiday
without your smiling face,
and maybe I should be more pleased
you're in a better place.
You swear that you are happy now
and never felt more free.
Well, I don't call this selfishness,
but what's in it for me?
Everytime I see a kiss,
it makes me miss you more.
Everytime I see a warm embrace,
it's like before
when many times, I wondered how
your life was treating you.
And then I'd call, or you'd come by.
Then all was good as new.
Chin-deep in depression, though,
is where I find myself;
wallowing in loneliness.
Just pictures on a shelf
remind me of the love we shared.
It seems so long ago,
yet time won't heal my shattered heart,
and why, I'll never know.

I spent another holiday
without your caring words.
It seemed no matter what our moods,
the fact was once we heard
each other's take on daily life,
we both then felt relieved
that things would be much better soon.
It's what we both believed.
You're not just missed for minutes,
like a moment here or there;
and yes, I have the memories.
It's like you're everywhere.
But that's just it: a memory . . .
in all I say and do.
And they don't fill this empty hole.
I need the real you.
You longed to be a mom while I
was proud to be your dad;
allowing us experiences
we both had never had.
You spent your time devoted to be
all that you could be.
But then God stuck His hand in
and stole you away from me.

He knew He'd have you for forever.
Why the sudden call?
All my questions go unanswered.
Was it worth it all?

I spent this joyless holiday
without your loving soul.
It's been almost a year now,
yet I still can't get control.
We both looked forward to a life of,
one day, growing old.
But snatching you away from me
has left me feeling cold.
Where's the joy in memories
when questions still remain?
We're taught to learn from life's quick blows.
With death, what did I gain?
I lost my one-and-only child.
You'll never be replaced,
and sorrow, tears, and loneliness
are all that I can taste.
Countless hours I've cried without
a clear path what to do;
Caught up in the turmoil of
how much I'm missing you.

I could go ballistic and let
falls count anywhere.
I could try the deep end
and see if someone is there.
Perhaps I'm done. I should just leave
this sad and sorry world.
Perhaps I shouldn't be like this,
but damn, I miss you, girl.

I must say I never felt lonely as a child growing up, and actually relished being alone. There is no one around to discredit you or have any problem with whatever you decide. That is a great opportunity for maturity to blossom.

Having friends is a blessing most people receive in their lives. But no amount of friends will do when you are needing that one special person. That is when you truly feel lonely.

THE DARKENING . . . THE AWAKENING

His riches were great and according to plan
seemingly the envy of most any man.
He had a great family . . . a sweet, loving wife;
fulfilling their dreams in a wonderful life.
The children were young and a fun-loving sort,
enjoying huge boxes made into a fort.
Happy and healthy, it pleased them to share
and be there for others, and no matter where.
It all seemed so easy to bring out the smiles,
but like any good thing, they last just awhile.

THE DARKENING . . .

The sudden 180 made no sense at all.
He felt he was banging his head on a wall.
But this was a wall that had been built for years;
just hidden with smiles and wiped-away tears.
He searched for assurance that it could be saved;
discovering love's on streets—two-way and paved.
No, this bitterness was a stubborn, vile hate
that hid something dark he could not contemplate;
for they were illusions. His frown turned to tears
as he tried preparing for darkening fears.
He felt his heart broken in so many ways,
and it then affected his mind everyday.

Him spiraling downward was how he would go
with therapy worthless. To pills, he said no.
It all still was nonsense. His life fell apart,
but there was one person still deep in his heart.
He still had his daughter. She'd stood by his side,
and told him he'd soon learn to smooth out the ride.
And then he accepted he'd done all he could;
remained calm and loyal, and his word was good.
He realized his life would take more sudden turns,
like losing his job, his home, and health concerns.
That's when the worst happened. He lost his ally.
So he crawled in a hole and wanted to die.

The darkest of fears had found him schizoid.
His heart and his soul seemed totally devoid.
His spirit depleted, he had nothing left.
He felt he had witnessed God's mistaken theft.
His plans with his daughter had now gone awry.
So he crawled in a hole and wanted to die.

His musing was gift-wrapped with regret and woe,
where tears were the ribbons and anger, the bow.
His life now in turmoil, he no longer slept.
Perhaps it was Evil that somehow had crept
deep into the thinking. Whatever the cause,
his life filled up with insurmountable flaws.

Friends offered help but it just made him cry.
So he crawled in a hole and wanted to die.

THE AWAKENING . . .

Does one ever know what will make a heart turn?
You might read the leaflets, but how can one learn
their lover has chosen to let their love fade;
forgetting past lessons from mistakes they made.
Reluctance, covertness, and faking heartache
become the new norm for the actions they take.
Love should stay patient and far from unkind,
just harder to show in these difficult times.
Though anger and vengeance may rise to the top,
know once they get started, they're so hard to stop.
Just look at it this way . . . don't fall in that trap
nor lower yourself to show all that bull crap.
You once called it love, but that's all in the past.
Now, use it for strength, and by sharper contrast,
a comforting peace and true love is revealed
to broaden horizons if only you yield.
'Cause when it's all over and you're left alone,
your character's something you have all your own.
The more that you tarnish, the less it will shine.
Most aren't really worth it, is what you will find.

Don't cry with the liars. They chose their own path.
They'll get their forever when facing God's wrath.

In all of our losses, there's often someone
who meant more than anything under the sun.
And that's where your focus and feelings should be
to gain truer insight and set your souls free.
Have faith your sweet angel is guiding you through
your last precious moments and all that you do.
But you must stay willing to keep your heart pure,
and you'll be rewarded with peace that endures.

Happiness and tranquility may be met with excruciating anxiety when they are discovered to have been false. However, they are easily discarded into an insignificant past when you understand deceitfulness. But when someone of value shows their worth with very little effort, it is an enlightening jolt to reality. Treasure those in your lives that have been there through all your struggles . . . and asked for nothing in return, but deserved everything. Those are the true angels of this world.

ONE YEAR AGO

A light bulb flickered late last night.
I thought you had come home.
I knelt and prayed "I missed you, girl.
I hate it here alone."
But it was not to be, my dear.
A faulty switch, it seemed
had broken silence in the dark
to wake me from my dream.
Some might decide their head held high
will hide this dreaded pain;
while all their silent suffering
is toxic to their brain.
But I will not withdraw my heart.
I'll wear it on my sleeve;
and mourn the day God forced His hand,
commanding you to leave.
Just like a thief comes in the night,
God stole without remorse.
Without a warning, all our plans
came to a halt. Of course,
I would have fought Him all the way.
It's just what fathers do.
I'm not naive. He would have won.

But I'd have fought for you.

The date was just one year ago,
God ripped my heart from me.
He eased your pain and suffering
and calmly set you free.
I still fight with that everyday.
Your pain was that intense.
But feeling helpless made this wound
that's festered ever since.
Oh Kellie, you were 24
and had your little boy;
and just like you had done for me,
he brought you tons of joy.
He can't begin to count his tears.
He knows his mommy's gone;
and still the anguish is relentless
for me every dawn.
Can someone understand this pain?
They haven't got a clue.
They hide awhile behind their smiles
with all they say and do.
I'm glad you're safe and pain-free now
since God took you away.
For me, the turmoil hasn't stopped.
It's torture everyday.

Most fathers feel responsible,
no matter what the cost.
I wish we'd changed the way things were
before your life was lost.
But since you now know all the facts,
my truth is crystal-clear.
And I should maybe feel relieved
that you were such a dear.

But for me now, it's still a blur.
It's cloudy through these tears.
My wounded soul and shattered heart
will last through all my years,
'cause I know it's impossible
to fill your angel shoes.
I just feel like God said to me,
"I'm taking her. You lose!"

These poems are similar to mini-movies that just play over and over inside the head, heart, and soul. I would prefer not to have had the experiences to write them, but perhaps they are a benefit to you.

THE POETIC DIARY

I started a booklet when she was first born;
just made up of excerpts and pages I'd torn
from this spiral notebook and that journal there.
No clues whatsoever how much we might share.
You see, I had always thought one little girl
would make my life special; completing my world.
Remembering feelings from near 12 years old;
at 14, I'd named her, if the truth be told.
But it took another . . . almost 13 years,
to welcome her presence, sans worries or fears.
She was, to be honest, the girl in my dreams.
Is anything, ever though, all that it seems?
In this case, a definite "yes" must be said.
My heart was transformed when I saw her in bed.
And then when I held her and touched her soft hair,
it so overwhelmed me 'cause she was right there.
My sweet baby daughter, my dear Kellie Rai,
had given me purpose that late winter day.

So as inspirations from her came to light,
I'd write several pages well into the night.
Expressions flowed freely. A phrase in my head
from her normal actions seemed worth being read.
Compelled, once I took her and we shared our day,

to retell our pleasures in more rhyming ways.
I wrote of us dancing and movies she liked.
I wrote of her swimming and riding her bikes.
I wrote how she'd laugh when I tickled her ribs;
of her changing table, and her in her crib.
We'd rewrite her research she needed for school,
and singing with Britney proved she sounded cool.
Yes, "Wavy" from "Crazy" by Miss Britney Spears,
got her admiration and praise from her peers.
To add tunes to poems seemed simple, and hey,
she never had problems receiving the "A."
I must admit writing for her was a breeze;
but writing ABOUT her put me more at ease.
I wrote of her travels and beauty contests,
and eighteen awards she won doing her best.
Like videos frozen in time with no tears,
I kept all these poems together for years.
They're not like a picture that fades over time;
their mem'ries are vivid and stay in their prime.

Some places we loved were the local bookstores.
We'd listen to music, share stories, and more.
I'd known for some time that I needed a book.
It had to be special, so we took a look.
I said "Find a journal that's special to you.
I'll write in some poems you'll wanna' read, too."

Covered with angels, her choice was quite thick.
I thought there is no way I'll finish this quick.
But since she had picked it out all by herself,
I couldn't return it to some lonely shelf.
So we went and bought it. It didn't take long
to fill up those pages with poems and songs.
I couldn't believe she inspired me so.
I'd grab pen and paper, and my mind let go.
The words just poured out like a syrupy goo.
To make them all rhyme seemed so easy to do.
Without realizing it, she was my muse,
and I was rejoicing while sharing the news.
But what made it special, or what seemed to me,
most poems had comments on their history.
It became a poetic diary, which made
it capture more memories; never to fade.

Those 100 pages, all written by hand,
became something special few would understand.
But Kellie had sensed what that book meant to me,
so I vowed she'd have it eventually.
It shared raw emotions. It was hard to read.
Such words at the wrong time can likely impede.
I kept it protected. She took it sometimes,
and when things were quiet, read it line by line.
I knew it had touched her. That was my intent.

My heart was so happy she knew what she meant.
It started discussions that we could pursue.
The bond it created was honest and true.
And then she'd return it. She had to be sure
until she could keep it, I'd keep it secure.

But God threw a big monkey wrench in our plans,
and called her home early. I don't understand.
I wrote it for her. By my vow, to abide,
I opened her casket and placed it inside.
I'm sure up in Heaven, this book they'll allow,
and since there's no tears, she'll enjoy it now.
It's still hard describing all she meant to me.
Perhaps I've succeeded, poetically.

She definitely deserved to have her presence felt for more than 24 short years to more than just the people she met. Perhaps, she will be proud of this one. The book mentioned above is a touching tribute to our relationship. Now, I am glad she has that angel journal she picked out and enjoys sharing it with Mom and the other angels.

EXPOSING NERVES

If saying goodbye was that easy,
my heart would be feeling less pain.
If comfort was dangling off doorknobs,
I'm sure that I would have remained.
Surrounded by anguish and silence,
I muddle through sorrow and hurt.
Attempts to break free go unnoticed,
so to this black hole I revert.
Since you were welcomed up in Heaven,
my life just keeps spiraling down.
Although you're still watching my efforts,
I've given you reasons to frown.
It's hard to climb out of depression,
with pills and drink never a choice.
They'd only add more to confusion,
and God isn't using His voice.
It's just the years we spent together,
this father will never forget.
My daughter, I'll love you forever,
and I haven't given up yet.

I've written so much since your passing—
compelled in through turmoil and tears.
If writing's to help bring some closure,

too bad. That's not happened in years.
To share is still difficult for me.
It feels like exposing a nerve.
Writing brings no sort of healing.
So really . . . whom best does it serve?
It's just that somewhere deep inside me,
these words seem to scream let them out.
Despite the hurt and better judgement,
they work well to cover my doubt.
When God wrapped this gift that He gave me,
I think He used too many bows.
It's taken years of desperation
to come to grips with all the woes.
Maybe somewhere hidden out there,
a person in need feels relief
by finding some comfort in reading
my words, where I describe my grief.

One poem that we wrote together,
I'm turning now into a book.
It should be on store shelves by Christmas.
I hope that you'll like how it looks.
The girl in the book looks lots like you
when you had just turned age 13.
The publisher's even excited.
It's "one of the best" that they've seen.

So I should pull myself together,
and somehow turn this thing around.
Or crawl in a room with the door closed
and never again make a sound.
The up and down options seem endless.
It's hard to know which way to go.
The lack of some closure weighs heavy
and feels like a boxing KO.
It may seem so easy for others.
They say it's past time to move on.
But how can I put back together
my shattered heart since you've been gone?

This is another of those where the mind drifts, stumbles, and seemingly falls into an abyss of torment, loneliness, and heartfelt pain. It is an unwilling journey, taken by a soul striving for answers.

REAL TEARS

I write down some words in amazement
at how much the phrases are true.
It's never been my main intention
to share all my feelings with you.
But sometimes, emotions win over
and can't be restrained nor held back.
Emotions this raw can't be altered.
It's like they go on the attack.
They cry out for fervent attention,
demanding they take center stage.
And that's when, with waterworks flowing,
come memories of your tender age
at how, when you were just a baby,
you cried for attention and care.
And no matter what I was doing,
my priority was "Be there!"

But those tears you cried as an infant
were just because you couldn't talk;
meaningful, yes, but not heartfelt,
like later, once you learned to walk.
And I had no problem relieving
the level of stress that you felt.
It seemed like a father's sworn duty

as into your eyes I would melt.

And then, as you got a bit older,
I counted my blessings each day.
Your laughter was so overwhelming,
all tensions would just float away.
It's like our initial connection
was made without question or pause.
It seemed such a natural occurrence
and backed by a heavenly cause.
The tears that you cried were so rare that
they disappeared as they began.
I felt like the luckiest father
and did not care to understand.
The tears cried from being spoiled rotten
and somehow not getting your way,
are more from gross manipulation,
and will catch up with you someday.

So crying was never an option.
Real tears rarely entered our life.
It's not we were cold or unfeeling.
It's more we just laughed away strife.
We had each other and we knew it.
No one could destroy our bond.
We had our whole lives there before us;

in through the abyss and beyond.
God's master plan never was factored.
Our lives were too rich to include
His changes to alter our plans to
destruction of this magnitude.
You might think a strong, assured parent
would never feel torturing pain.
But losing the life of a loved one
can weigh heavily on the brain.
My eyes slowly fill up with teardrops
as sadness and hurt overwhelms.
I must find inevitable closure
when facing impossible realms.
My heart cries out daily with anguish
and bathes my pierced soul with real tears.
I'm blind to the comfort and guidance
when facing uncompromised fears.
These tears can cause huge disappointments
and cause lack of focus and tact;
while battling the surging of demons
and trying to get back on track.

So here's my advice to some parents.
Cherish each day with your child.
They may fill their life with achievements
or only be here for awhile.

You never know. From this day forward,
no matter how busy you are,
quality time with your children
is most satisfying by far.

No one can dictate proper mourning
or what it can do for a soul.
Some will say "It's over. Forget it!"
while struggling to regain control.
But think for a second what got you
to that very moment in time.
The love that you shared and their passing
presented a true paradigm.
So why should your life now lose focus
when what's most important is gone?
It's just for that sheer fact exactly.
Tomorrow, your life can move on.

It struck me how many of our tears seem superficial within moments of drying them. But when your heart truly aches and your soul feels empty, those are real tears and cannot be wiped away or absorbed easily with a tissue.

THE HARDEST UNSPOKEN GOODBYE

The past five months have been nerve-racking,
with losing my daughter and all.
I'm facing increasing withdrawals
and some sort of bottomless fall.
I have to move out very shortly
and doubt I'll be back for some time.
But you're in my heart now forever,
and mem'ries of you fill my mind.
I know they're supposed to bring comfort;
reliving the past for awhile.
But nothing related to comfort
burns in my heart without your smile.
To think of my future without you
seems pointless and filled with despair.
I prayed for just one healthy daughter.
Was that so much more than was fair?

So I'm, once again, at your gravesite.
Though covered with clippings and cold,
I cleaned out each letter with Q-tips,
and suddenly felt very old.
I freshened your bouquet of flowers.
The purple and red are so bright.
You colored my life like a rainbow,

and made everything seem alright.
The Florida sun was not hiding,
and warmed up your stone to my touch.
And then again, tears started falling.
My Kellie, I miss you so much.

My beloved daughter, and mother
to Tyler who cries for his mom;
God stole you away from our clutches,
and hit like a nuclear bomb.
He robbed you of being a mother
and my thrill of helping you grow.
The time that we spent here was awesome,
but limited. How could we know?
My one chance of being a father
has basically gone up in flames.
The rage I am squelching with anger
does little to distort the blame.
Just knowing you're now gone forever
has taken my heart to new lows.
Dry solitude beckons my psyche,
where doubts and depression will grow.

No farewell words entered your eardrums.
No precious time spent on goodbyes.

You left before anyone knew it.
And only God answers the why.
But He's cut off communications,
allowing the pain to persist.
He's seemingly cool with His judgements,
and not caring how much you're missed.
My heart is still aching with sadness
as rivers of tears always flow.
There's so much I lost when He took you,
I'm sure no one will ever know.

I hear God awards Earthly passes
to angels who keep their wings fluffed.
To see you once more would be special,
though 90 times won't be enough.
I know God took you for a reason.
On birthdays, you still get a wish?
You'll probably ask for a kitten,
or maybe a bowl of goldfish.
And I wouldn't blame you for choosing
a pet that reminds you of here.
But I've got no plans for the weekend,
and I'd make a great souvenir.
'Cause facing each day is a burden,
but life must go on as we know.

Please ask that my sorrow be lessened
as up this hill, onward, I go.

On a flight from FL to MO by way of PA, I sat next to a teenage girl. After a few minutes of getting settled in, I had hoped to spend some precious minutes on my laptop. The girl had hoped to spend some time with her mp3 player. When we both realized our batteries were low, we struck up a conversation. She mentioned she loved music and enjoyed writing lyrics sometimes and poetry. She had a few in her notebook and shared them with me. When she said they were often a struggle to write, I assured her it would get easier as long as she was passionate and wrote from deep within. I shared with her a bit about my daughter Kellie, and explained that she had inspired me to write songs and many poems. When I told her sometimes they seem to write themselves, she asked me to write one before we landed in PA. I found a large scrap of paper, and my mind went to my visit at Kellie's grave the day before. Before landing, the above poem was written.

MY HUMAN ANGEL

God brings 20,000 kids to Heaven everyday.
It's hard for them to walk and talk; and some can't even play.
They're not up there to float around . . . what kind of life is that?
He needs a bunch of angels to put on their day care hat.
20,000 needy children are an awful lot.
Multiply that by the days and this is what you've got—
multitudes of single children waiting to be held
and nurtured by a caring group where love's unparalleled.
Since it's up in Heaven, there's no screams nor crying tears;
just lots of thoughtful angels working hard to calm their fears.

I know my daughter, Kellie, had found her perfect job.
She had her baby, Tyler, and loved being a mom.
Her school career had ended. She'd moved on with her life.
But losing her in silence cut through me like a knife.
God had a caring future planned for my baby girl,
and sent her down to share in my tiny, carved out world.
But was it just for practice? A few short joy-filled years?
My heart cries out for comfort in ways that no one hears.
He gave us to each other in ways I won't forget.
But why He had to take her . . . I haven't solved that yet.
I can't dwell on her passing. It seems like yesterday.
But also like forever, I've had to face each day
with knowing she's not with me. I miss her face and voice.
And it keeps my heart bleeding to know I had no choice.

She had a way about her I'd never seen before,
and I felt many blessings, 'til she turned 24.

She had a special aura that touched my very soul.
For her, it took no effort. That kept me in control.
My quarter-century with her seems now, just like a day.
We thought we had a future, but God stole her away.
Perhaps, He had some bigger plans for her up there.
Hey, she was MY daughter, so I don't really care.
She was MY human angel, deserving of more time
to spend HERE with her family, and fortunes still to find.
He thought she wasn't happy and brought her home to Him?
He must have not been looking . . . she always had a grin.
He gets her for forever, but still I wonder why
He took her from her baby and made him have to cry.
Memorial Day weekend: while many congregate,
two years ago she left here, so I won't celebrate.
She said she's never sad there, so I must trust her word.
But my last goodbye to her is one she never heard.

I researched to find out just how many children God calls to Heaven each and every day. It is hard to believe how much grief that causes those of us left behind. Perhaps even harder to believe is just how little most people believe it has to do with them.

A TIME TO MOURN

Some people say six months is plenty,
while others say maybe a year,
when mourning the loss of a loved one
and finish the shedding of tears.
The therapists say medication
will help you get over the hump.
Sorry, but pills are addictive,
and we're talking more than a bump.
I know many people have done it;
'cause losing a loved one is hard.
We're all taught to cherish our fam'lies;
protect them and keep up our guard.
And yes, maybe a distant cousin
does not pull the heartstrings that much.
Perhaps no love's lost between siblings
or parents with whom we've lost touch.
The family that we're born into;
we have not one ounce of control.
The Man Upstairs makes those decisions
and writes them on some secret scroll.
So maybe six months is sufficient
to dry up the tears and move on.
They'll spend their forever in Heaven.

So, somehow, they're not really gone.

But try to tell that to a Father
whose deepest of wishes came true
when he first held his baby daughter,
and loved her more each day she grew.
Try telling him she's very happy
to be with the angels on high;
that he needs to focus on living
and find other reasons to cry.
Try telling him he has the mem'ries
of all that she did while alive.
And talking about it does wonders,
but he must move on to survive.

You know his reaction? I'll tell you.
And it's not to sound crass nor crude.
But that fateful day was life-changing.
Suggesting it's over is rude.
'Cause losing a daughter so precious,
without any warning or cause,
it eats at the mind like a virus;
with rarely a moment of pause.
A mere broken heart would be comfort,
since his is now shattered and smashed.

Nothing compares to this anguish.
He feels his whole life has been trashed.
And then there's his soul. That one's tricky.
Suffice it to say there's a hole
that seems a mile wide in the middle;
with no clue on how to be whole.
The pastors and preachers will tell him
the Bible has comforting words.
True . . . it has healed many thousands,
but mostly malarkey, he's heard.

Stubborn and lost in his sorrow?
Perhaps that's a fair estimate.
All the more need for compassion,
or later you battle regret.

He paints on a smile through the struggle
of facing the dawn of each day.
The pain and the torment are endless.
He prays they would just fade away.
But all of his prayers go unanswered.
His questions for closure remain.
That fateful day plays like a record;
repeating again and again.

I'll never suggest someone finish
their mourning in some length of time.
The personal feelings they harbor
are surely no business of mine.
I'll just try to offer compassion
and share with them what I've been through.
I understand their heart is shattered.
Someday, that someone could be you.

Some people that have lost a LOVED one get what this is like. However, this poem stemmed from most of them that don't. It involves putting yourself in their shoes if necessary, and most people, including friends and family, are afraid or unwilling to do that.

ADORNING HEAVEN

Another birthday, come and gone,
but never what was meant
to be the way to celebrate
your special day. We spent
a bunch of years, each one unique,
remembering your day;
but had no clue the 27th
would be spent this way.
When each November 21st arrived,
it seemed to me
to be a lot like Christmas Day.
The reasons that would be
were gifts and decorations.
'Cause within that rigmarole
was God had blessed me with a child
that touched my very soul.
Plus, your presence filled my heart
with joy on those days.
For proof, you heard my many words
like Ernest Hemingway's.
He kept a notepad at his side.
With me, I had your ears,
and shared them with you many times

throughout your growing years.

I don't regret not writing down
some poems you inspired,
although, more DVD's of us,
since then, I have desired.
If only to have more of you,
I taped us quite a lot
while dancing in the living room;
much better than snapshots.
But maybe up in Heaven now,
my old rhymes still ring true;
along with all the angels' songs
expressing love for you.
I'm not sure just how young you look.
That's never been made clear.
So fluff your wings and tell me soon,
or send the Rocketeer.
"The Rock-a-who?" You made me laugh
whenever we would watch
those films where you would mimic lines
and graded as top-notch.
My mind can only speculate
just how you spend your times,
but it would melt this father's heart
if some are with my rhymes.

You have to know I miss you
with each ticking of the clock;
and though two years have passed,
I still deal with the aftershock.
Now I don't mean to ramble on;
the phrases come like this.
That's why they write themselves so quickly
when I reminisce.
Maybe you watch over children,
taking time to share
the human part of your existence,
showing that you care.
Perhaps they're looking forward to
the lessons you bestow
since God called them home early also
before they could grow.
Well, if while you're adorning Heaven,
they want your review,
share with them this special love
your father had for you.

This is pure loneliness over another special day come and gone and speculation of what is and what could have been.

WHEN I GET UP TO HEAVEN

It's been a long time coming
for this anguish to subside.
I've talked with God and angels,
but I'm still unqualified
to find out all the answers
as to why you had to go.
I'm often still beside myself,
so healing has been slow.

When I get up to Heaven,
I'll be glad to see your face.
When I get up to Heaven,
you'll be glad to show your place.
You'll live in a white mansion
with a glowing purple fence
with green and purple flowers
growing on it. Ever since
you made your way to Heaven,
I am sure your needs were met.
And that includes your spirit
and a kitten for a pet.

By now, you'll have met Tiger
with his legs as good as new.
And he will be so loving
as he gets to know you, too.
He had a long life down here
while I was just a boy.
The bus sent him to Heaven;
now he gets to bring you joy.
I'm sure you'll like his purring,
though his fur won't be as long.
And he is independent,
but he'll never do you wrong.

The books in the libraries
tell us we can speculate
on what it's like where you are,
but that's just to estimate
a knowledge from opinions
reading that book or this scribe.
I just know it's more awesome
than they've vividly described.
Harps may be in abundance.
Each hill may have singing choirs
with special guest performances—
celebs that we admired.

These books describe archangels.
They may claim the streets are gold.
But since you left, my daughter,
my heart still is bleeding cold.

So what's important to me
is not what's past Heaven's gate;
'cause for a short time only
are we there to congregate.
No, what's much more important
is the journey after that:
when we're all joined together
. . . and you get to keep your cat.

This was another of those poems that literally poured out and begged
to be written down. Kellie loved cats and I felt her presence while writing
this rhyme. It also may be one of those that keeps growing. We shall see.

LETTER TO GOD

You have the pow'r to take me, God;
the pow'r to bring me home.
You know I'd rather be up there
than down here all alone.
But since You've left me down here still
to face the dawn each day,
I'll try to trust Your master plan
and find out as I pray.
I'll ask for strength to guide me through
these overwhelming fears.
I'll ask for clarity and wisdom
in my coming years.
I'll ask for understanding why
I can't hold back my tears,
and ask for inner peace with all
my cries that no one hears.

I trust You're keeping Kellie busy
and she's filled with joy.
Heaven may lack sadness,
but she still misses her boy.
You ripped an angel from us
while Your mansions there are filled;
ignoring all our heartfelt plans

and lives we tried to build.
I try to understand how You
can justify all this,
but can't get past Your war
with Satan when I reminisce.
To be waist-deep in battle,
yet still find a soul to love,
is only 'cause we listened to
Your guidance from above.
To give such love so freely
is so easy with a child.
Your son and ten commandments
teach us to be meek and mild.
You also gave us brains
and curiosities to solve.
So why then should I wait
until I finally dissolve?

I don't need some religious leaders'
far-fetching beliefs;
nor climb a mountain through the clouds
nor summon Indian chiefs.
'Cause if they had the answers
and they really knew what's right,
they'd be discussing virtues
and not be inclined to fight.

Dare I delve into all the problems
with some things they say?
Attending seminars and studies
helped them find Your way?
Of course not. They still argue
over if You sent Your son.
And scientists still bicker about
how we've all begun.
They have the right to be informed
or kick back and relax.
Such little proof is needed
validating artifacts.
No, mostly cults and strict believers
haven't got a clue.
The common thread that joins us others
is we're seeking You.

And some of us can't sit to watch
Your master plan unfold.
We seek more understanding.
Give us something to behold.
We're ready and united,
standing tall in Your brigade.
Show us where our God is
and the promises You made.
Prove to these lost causes
what they think they learned so well.
Unleash Your holy wrath that sends
these demons straight to Hell.

This may alter Your timeline
of restructuring this world,
but, God, I'm just a father
trying to get home to my girl.

The irony of a letter to God is that He already knows a person's heart and what they want to say before they clarify it to write it down. But with that also comes the knowledge that sometimes a person feels compelled to just put those thoughts into words. And the truth is, after letting numerous "poetic" thoughts drift away during my youth, I have felt compelled to write these down. Some I have saved for my eyes only. This one, at this time, I feel compelled to share.

No Sleep For The Weary

BABIES

Babies are handfuls of troublesome goo.
Do you think that's somehow referring to you?
No, my baby Kellie, you're nothing like that;
but more like a princess who doesn't get fat.
You might wake up crying, but that's still ok;
coddling you is the best part of my day.
I'll feed you and clean you, then take off your bib,
and if you get sleepy, lay you in the crib.
Your crib is quite spacious and colorful, too.
I put it together especially for you.
But your changing table required more tools
and knowledge I'd gotten from jobs and in schools.
I wanted it sturdy, but soft to your touch.
I wanted it roomy for diapers and such.
I wanted all messes to be kept contained,
and highly unlikely to absorb a stain.
Transforming a cabinet, I lowered a shelf;
then got some soft leather to tack on myself.
It has shelves for storage installed underneath,
and even a pocket for tooth fairy teeth.
To clamp on a mobile is easy enough,
or changing a diaper, then lotion or puff.

But soon, you'll outgrow them and no longer need
diapers for changing and soft books to read.
That suits me just fine 'cause I'm anxious to see
the wonderful choices you make due to me.

This is one of those poems that I had not seen for a long time and was not in Kellie's poetic diary. It is probably only the 2nd or 3rd poem I wrote for her.

Kellie's changing table was a project I put lots of work into and was very proud of it. I altered a cabinet by recessing a shelf down into it to make it safe and then covering it with a soft, easy-to-clean leather fabric. I designed shelves for underneath so as to make it compact and very practical. Just knowing it was for Kellie made it worth all the effort.

THE SOULS OF MAN

Once a soul makes it to Heaven,
does it always stay?
Or does God put it in a babe
to live the human way?
Some folks say they've lived past lives.
Well, I believe it's true.
'Cause God can use an angel here
for what He wants to do.
Imaginations may run wild
and you can voice your view;
but when the claims are from a child,
you're swayed toward it's true.
We all know Satan has his demons.
God's counterattack
must be He sends His angels here
when all we see is black.
They're picked to give a rescued soul
a chance for his reprieve
and offer up a little hope
to those who don't believe.
Maybe this soul once belonged
to a religious sect
that misinterpreted the Word

and had a bad effect.
Maybe someone's lost their way
because of circumstance.
A guiding angel from above
gives them another chance.
Heaven's full of angels that have
lived since time began,
and now we have this Holy War
which fights for souls of Man.
I won't waste time to speculate
and tell you how to be.
Since we all have a choice to make,
I'll choose what's best for me.

After all these years of writing, I am still not sure where some of these poems comes from. But I do appreciate the opportunity to share some of the chosen ones, and I hope searching hearts are touched in special ways because of them.

RUBY—A TRUE GEM

Sometimes jewels sparkle.
Some, you're proud to show.
And when they hit the light just right,
they cast an awesome glow.
Some shine on with brilliance,
whether green or blue.
But none of them have qualities
like this rare gem I knew.

No, it's not a crystal;
nor a piece of jade.
The special gem was Ruby and
the best God ever made.
Her smile was endearing,
and her gentle voice
outshone all other qualities
when Marvin made his choice.

What was most impressive,
in my younger years,
though strict, she had a gentle heart
and never showed her fears.
Her love for Christ Jesus
and her faith in God,

gave to her life a moral guide
some folks would think was odd.
But her entire fam'ly
and the kids they've raised,
were quick to show that lessons learned
were rooted in God's praise.

Sunday service singing
had angelic flair.
She lead the gospel melodies
with notes that danced on air.
Filled with fascination,
I learned how to sing.
And then an idea came to me
just earlier this Spring.
A few weeks of practice
with no microphone,
made me agree to Cheryl's dare.
"Where No One Stands Alone,"
Cheryl played perfectly,
while I sang my rhyme;
expressing our deep gratitude
while we still had some time.

This gem—Ruby Edwards:
Finley, as a child,

always displayed such honesty
and rarely strayed from mild.
Now she's gone to Heaven.
Brightening her smile,
she's looked so forward to this day;
although we'll cry awhile.
The heavenly ensembles
are fortunate to get
this new lead to inspire who
joins Kellie for duets.

Mill Creek was there for her.
She gave so much more.
And she's received eternal peace
from her Lord and Saviour.
Loved ones mourn her passing.
Now she's good as new.
If you were blessed to know this saint,
you were affected, too.
Thank you so much, Ruby.
Your sparkle lights the skies;
diminishing the nearby stars to
reflect in my eyes.

This special lady was the epitome of a Christian and she never strayed from those beliefs as a child and a mother. I was fortunate to have several opportunities to have Kellie meet Ruby when we would go to church. She also remarked what a nice lady Ruby was and how well she could sing.

THE FEELING OF LOVE

When you finally meet the one of your dreams,
how can you fathom an immeasurable thing?
How can you fault a perfection of grace,
or not long for more with one warm embrace?
Is it not impossible to try to endure,
when feeling emotions so strong and so pure?
This feeling is happy, patient, and kind,
but to be mutual, takes more than time.
The gentle caresses and passionate nights,
stem from this feeling where everything's right.
We're blessed with a nugget—this gift from above,
in its purest form, is the feeling of love.

This was one of my first poems and has lots of potential to be much longer and with greater detail. If the muse strikes, I will see what I can do. Kellie liked that it was about love.

"ENLIGHTENED JOURNEYS"

Including "There's A Raccoon In My Bedroom," "Life," and "Eve's New Year's Eve (First Love)"

(COMING IN 2014)

THERE'S A RACCOON
IN MY BEDROOM!

A raccoon in my bedroom?
OMG! He'll rip my clothes
I've laundered and just folded.
I've been beating out my throws.
Is he behind the dresser?
You're too scared? Just shine the light!
He may be cute and cuddly,
but he's not spending the night.
If I peer in the closet,
I should see his beady eyes.
And no, the mask they wear is
not some sort of smart disguise.
I can't deal with a raccoon.
I've got . . . oh, it's just a joke?
You read that post on Facebook?
Oh, they're all such friendly folks.

Confess to liking porn? I
hardly think that's food for thought;
and looking for used sex toys?
That's not something that I aught.
You said you smoked some crack today?
Girl, have you lost your mind?
Oh my, scanning Facebook posts,

you never know what you'll find.
I don't do drugs like cocaine.
Never cheated on an ex.
Again, I don't watch pornos
and I don't need toys for sex.
My marriage lasted 60 years.
I never cared to cheat.
Now, how about you turn that off?
It's almost time to eat.

I didn't fall in vomit
at McDonald's yesterday.
In fact, I had a burger
and some fries and iced latte.
Obamacare fiascoes
have been raging now for months;
so I don't think a third term
will be likely for a dunce.
And how can you be pregnant?
If you change into a man,
then that would solve that problem.
If you want, I guess you can.

You need time for chillaxin'?
Hon, your clothes need put away.
And all the coons are outside,

so enough of that today.
These comments are sheer nonsense.
I've got better things to do.
But if you want some dinner,
I suggest you help me, too.

The phrase for the last poem struck me as funny when I first saw it online. Growing up on a farm, cornering a raccoon was not usually an ideal situation, especially if it was in your house. Now, the phrase has gone viral and many are getting in on the game. I researched it and after reading a few articles, this poem started to formulate in my mind. I imagined a grandmother having an anxiety attack with a granddaughter like Kellie. Must have been a slow day . . . Anyway, trends come and go and who knows how long this one will last. To some, it may be mostly a fond memory like the Pet Rock or Chia Pet, or be forever ingrained into our culture like Bootylicious and OMG! Oops! Gotta' go. There's a raccoon in my . . .

LIFE

The trials that we go through
with each and every day
should only make us stronger.
Well, yeah! That's what they say.
But struggles, dodging bullets,
and clawing our way through
should mean much more than headaches.
We should have found the clues
to help us reach that peaceful,
and everflowing stream,
enlightening our senses,
fulfilling all our dreams.
Imagining a mountain
and how to reach the top,
we wonder if we'll make it,
or may be forced to stop.
Whether in a valley,
or high atop a hill,
we mostly long for comfort;
to feel we've been fulfilled.

But how to go about this?
We ponder this a lot:
a whole lifetime of offers,
and if we should or not.

We may look here for shortcuts,
or there for ins and outs;
forgetting that the journey
is what it's all about.
Yet many do choose shortcuts
and focus on one thing
they think will solve all problems
while earning the brass ring.

They choose to build their body
with muscles strong as steel.
With strength and exercising,
they're more than apt to feel
the pride and love they're after.
A sexy, tall physique
is on the lips of many.
It seems that's all they seek.
They may work hard at fitness,
but often when they do,
it's all that holds their interest.
They cease to care for you.

But if it's not the body,
then what about the mind?
With current brain enhancements,
more problems you will find.
But if it's just brain power,
where wisdom is the key;
and answering hard questions
is where you want to be,
intelligence is crucial
to get you through the day.
But think for just a second.
Is it the only way?
Can we get through life's trials
with just a high IQ?
Well, if you try, you'll find out
there's more you need to do.

Ok, there's still religion
that some say guide your way.
And they will recite scriptures
they study every day.
But yet, they still will struggle
with many basic things,
and ridicule their brethren
with vicious words that sting.

Now if that's your intention . . .
you think that's all you need?
I'll gasp for one mere second;
then bring you up to speed.
Your body strength will leave you
and tricks betray your mind.
And fighting for religions
is not the way to find
that peace and understanding
we all are searching for.

It's something we are born with
that helps unlock the door.
Your mind can't move a mountain,
but one rock at a time
can be moved with your muscles.
And that's when you will find
that as your muscles weaken,
your brain says "Let's do more."
And by working together,
you'll find the choice of doors
that leads to satisfaction
of body, mind, and soul.
You just have to be willing
to give God the controls.

Ask for strength and guidance;
accepting that your fate
you choose is mediocre.
God's plan for you is great.
And if religious leaders
are causing you to stray,
wrestle back your freedoms
and God will light your way.

The roads behind are winding,
and long and often rough.
It's just as God has promised—
to give us just enough
to get us through temptations
we find along the road.
His way is straight and narrow
but with a heavy load.

The wondrous gifts He gives us
are wrapped in loving care.
It's something deep within us.
You'll know it when it's there.
But that's not all He gives us.
For when we do His will,
we're given friends and loved ones
to also help until

we get to where we're headed.
And destiny awaits,
rewarding us with treasures
beyond the pearly gates.

To have a friend support you,
when trials have you down
can be a welcome shoulder,
and change that weary frown
into a steady smile that
can brighten any heart.
Depression knows no begging.
It's up to friends to start
to recognize the heartache
and prove they really care;
remembering, when troubled,
that trusted friend was there.
Each step of life's tall ladder,
that someone's gonna' climb,
is strong and then supportive
for one step at a time.
A friend will lift you higher
and pump you full of pep,
as you move up and onward
with each successful step.

The mountaintop is waiting.
The valley's lush and green.
And with true love and friendships,
the prettiest you have seen.
So don't let all the struggles
somehow do you in.
Just learn from all the past mistakes
and rise to start again.

These are some of the many of the "enlightened journeys" I have taken, and learning the destination is always a mystery. The quest is to make it interesting and always worthy of facing another day.

EVE'S NEW YEAR'S EVE

Eve fell in love while very young,
just barely past a child.
This love was new and strange to her,
but still it made her smile.
She'd sneaked away to several parties
in her prior years,
and they were always filled with laughter;
rarely any tears.
It made her feel like she belonged,
so safe and warm and good,
and all her friends were happy too.
She wondered if she would
feel closer than she did right then
because it felt so right.
She'd never known true love before,
but when John held her tight,
she thought she'd melt into his heart
and never wanna' leave.
He'd be so handsome and sexy
this night on New Year's Eve.
But on this night, this night of nights,
God had made other plans.
And with fate knocking on their doors,

they wouldn't understand.

It started when John picked Eve up
to take her out to eat.
She'd tried on blouses and lace skirts
to wear for when they'd meet.
The sun was outside shining
as she'd laid among her clothes;
and thought "I must be crazy!
I would not wear this with those!"
She chose a ruffled lace white blouse
and pink jean mini-skirt
and it matched well his pleated pants
and green Armani shirt.
She was a feast there for his eyes,
just as she cracked the door,
and then he pushed it open wide,
and gushed as he saw more.
A few secluded spots they found
to make out while they drove.
He said "I need to get some things
before we hit 'The Grove.'"
With beer and condoms grabbed,
he quickly paid and got back in.
He leaned over and kissed Eve's cheek.
She gave him quite a grin.

Then at the restaurant, it was like
these two were all alone.
Their dreamy eyes and soft mood music
helped to set the tone.
Their laughs and giggles filled the booth.
His hand slid to her knee,
and as she looked into his eyes,
it dawned on her to be
there at the party before 10,
so they could all say "Hi."
And then just past the stroke of 12,
they both could say "Goodbye."
For she had just turned 17,
and felt she was in love.
And here he was, her manly hunk,
and all that she thought of.
She had decided six months back,
this night her life would change
and with a bit of sweet seduction,
she had then arranged
to follow through and give herself
and have him for all time,
for she knew that he wanted her
and was just shy and kind.
The only thing about it was

she hadn't told him yet,
but she had felt they formed a
special bond the day they met.

Eve left the restaurant glowing
as her plan was coming through.
She climbed into the backseat
and she knew just what to do.
While wiggling all her fingers
as she ran them down John's chest,
she nibbled on his ear and asked him,
"Which you like the best?"
Her hot breath hit his eardrum
and he nearly dropped his jaw;
but then they turned the corner
and the party house they saw.
They pulled up on the hillside
and then with a mighty yell,
"Let's get this party started!"
was so loud she almost fell.
But John's arms were there waiting
and he lifted her with ease.
And caught up in the moment,
she said, grinning, "Johnny please,
can we stay just an hour?
I've got better things in mind."

Then put her hips against him
as she gave a little grind.

When they got to the party,
it was really quite a sight.
The girls were flashing everywhere
and guys were high as kites.
Eve saw Tom in the corner, pouting.
Guess he'd failed again
with all his flirty antics
'cause his dream girl was a friend.
Evonne was quite the looker,
but Tom never got to boast
'cause she had made her mind up
who it was she wanted most.
And that was what infuriated Eve
and seared her core.
Evonne had spread the rumor
that she loved to be John's whore,
and Eve was just a plaything . . .
just a friend to pass the time.
Eve had no fear of battle.
She believed Evonne would find
that John could never love her
since he gave his heart away
a few months after meeting Eve

that rainy autumn day.

Well, that was now Eve's mindset
as she scanned the rowdy scene.
And then began to worry
as Evonne had not been seen.
She could be in a bedroom
upstairs doing all her tricks
with two or even three guys at a time.
It made her sick
to think that John had ever spent
a moment with that pile.
And then he bumped into her
with that ever loving smile.
"Are you ok?" he asked her,
as he sipped his cup of beer.
"Of course!" she strained to tell him
as she quickly hid her fear.
"I have to use the bathroom,"
she said, heading to the stairs.
Then took the room in slowly
as she gazed at all the pairs
of guys and girls caressing
in the corners, on the floor,
and on the chairs and couches.
A loud knock came from the door.

The door was thrown wide open
by the stoned Bartholomew.
And then the room went quiet
as Evonne came strutting through.
That girl was oozing sex appeal
like no one ever had,
and all the good guys wanted
for one night, just to be bad.
A thought kept nagging at Eve . . .
she again erased her mind.
And climbed the stairs to find a
dozen people there in line.
Her friend was slowly coming
out the door but seemed ok,
and asked Eve how much longer
it was she thought she would stay.
Eve couldn't hide her anger,
but told Lara of her plans
to make John come to grips
with what it takes to be her man.
Lara laughed. "You're crazy!
You're a naughty little girl!
You're like a little nut and
you want John to be your squirrel."
Now downstairs, Tom was

in the kitchen for another beer.
The fridge was almost empty,
but then he was cavalier
when turning, he saw beauty
unmatched in his wildest dream.
But Evonne didn't care and grabbed
two cans of whipping cream.
"Hey! Come on boys," she called out
to like everyone that heard.
Although Tom's temper flared up,
still he couldn't say a word.
He cursed his soul 'cause many times
he'd felt he'd had enough,
but then to dream without Evonne
had always been too tough.
He banged his fist and then looked up
to see John sneak upstairs.
And then a thought came to him
as he ran out in despair.
Eve exited the bathroom
moments later and then stopped,
as two girls walked right past her
with a long black riding crop.

She went back down the stairs to look
for John so they could leave,

for she had planned a special time
for them this New Year's Eve.
This party, with such foolishness,
was getting out of hand.
With her mom's curfew "out 'til two,"
she better find her man.
She thought she heard his laughter
coming from the lofty stairs.
She dashed around the corner
and looked up. He wasn't there.
A large crowd still was outside
so she combed through that awhile.
But still she couldn't find him,
so she asked his buddy, Kyle.
"Have you seen John out here?"
she asked, almost afraid to hear.
"Uhhh no," Kyle hesitated,
and then mumbled in her ear.
Her face got fiery red
as she ran down toward the street.
Then, crouched behind a bumper,
she could hear somebody's feet.

It was her buddy Tom and
he was talking really fast
about how much he loved Evonne

and how to make it last.
Eve stood up, took him by the arms
and stared into his eyes
and said, "She never loved you.
Surely you can't be surprised."
Tom stood there in amazement,
like that thought was somehow new,
but then to Eve, replied "Right!
I'll do what I gotta' do."
Eve sighed, and walked toward the party,
feeling somewhat dazed.
A naked girl climbed out a window.
Eve stood there amazed
and watched her on the roof in horror
as she almost fell.
Eve's mind was racing wildly,
so fast that she couldn't yell.
The girl then grabbed the sill, and wobbling,
slowly climbed back in,
and then amid the claps and cheers,
the year came to an end.

A guy came from the kitchen shouting
"Hey man, where's the beer?"
A girl checked out the pantry
and said "Bummer, nothing here."

Eve hadn't found John anywhere
and then she had a thought,
and quickly went down to the car
to get what John had bought.
She saw the beer was still there,
but the tiny bag was gone.
And then poor Eve remembered,
she had also seen Evonne;
but only at the door. She wondered,
"What is she up to?
That girl is always trouble,
but she'd sworn that she was through
with throwing herself at John
and the threat had somehow died."
Although Eve's heart hurt deeply,
and, at times, it made her cry.
Her mind again was racing
as she got out of the car;
then John jumped from the curb
and said "My god, Eve, there you are!"

A shot was heard inside the house
and then Tom stumbled out,
with Evonne close behind him shouting,
"What was that about?"
John left the car to grab him

and then laid him in the back.
Evonne then climbed inside
like some crazed nymphomaniac.
She placed her hand back on his side
and held his hand real tight,
and kept on whispering in his ear,
"You're gonna' be alright."
John started up the car
as Eve jumped in the other side
and half the crowd was laughing
as the drunk ones waved goodbye.
John ripped his shirt off quickly
and said "Hold against his hip!"
Eve said "This night's been crazy."
John said "What a freakin' trip!"
Then Tom let out a moan
and pulled his head from Evonne's lap,
and said "You think you got it bad?
Man, I feel like crap!"
Evonne then moved in closer;
put her finger to his mouth,
and whispered to him softly
with her right hand moving south.
Eve ripped a scarf from Evonne's hair
and said "Here Tom, use this!

I'm sure it will feel better
than a trashy worthless kiss!"
And with a huff, Evonne sat back
and glared right back at Eve.
These naive kids were facing
much more than they could conceive.
"Wait! Go this way!" Evonne yelled out.
"This road is shorter here!"
John swerved the car to make the turn,
but Eve's face filled with fear.
She looked to John for reassurance
that this way was best,
as Evonne slid her foot through sideways
to John's left armrest.
But John continued driving,
still an hour more or so.
The night was deathly dark and quiet;
just a faint moon glow.

Eve was fearful, also,
as she thought about her mom
and knew she'd soon be worried.
Then she turned around to Tom.
It seemed he'd been too quiet,
but just resting, she could see.
Evonne was gonna' touch him,

but Eve told her "Let him be!"
The sky was overcast and dreary.
Storms were moving in.
The four of them were on a road
that they had never been.
A railroad crossing up ahead
made John have to slow down.
Then Tom said he was feeling sick.
"Where is that ******* town?"
"Another 40 miles, I think,"
was all Evonne would say.
"Well, stop then, John. I gotta' puke!
I don't think I can wait."
"Oh come on, Tom. Are you for sure?
We're running out of time!"
said Eve. But then John pulled up
near the railroad crossing sign.

"I gotta' pee," Evonne said,
but her foot caught in John's door,
and Eve saw John ease back her leg.
But then Tom moaned before
Eve could say anything to John.
Tom needed help to move.
"I'll ask him later," Eve thought,
"since he has nothing to prove."

But Eve was only 17.
This "love" was new to her,
and nothing like her dad had taught.
Of that, she was for sure.
Just then a cloud cracked open
and the rain began to fall.
And in a few short minutes,
it had totally drenched them all.
Tom's moaning grew much louder
as Eve moved to comfort him,
then stood up, shocked, and furious
when she saw both of them.
Evonne had left the bushes
and was hitting on John hard,
and then yelled, "What about the night
we spent at the graveyard?
Have you forgotten all you told me?
She's nothing to you!"
Eve backed away, heartbroken,
feeling "What else can I do?"
She didn't beg for honesty,
for that would take too long.
And John, with his reactions,
proved to Eve she wasn't wrong.
Tom also heard the yelling

as he limped back to the car.
The two kept fighting, soaked,
and Eve thought, "This is so bizarre."
Evonne just kept on screaming
things they'd seemingly discussed,
while Eve kept staring through the rain
with wonder and disgust.
Foolishly, she'd always thought
he'd keep her safe and warm.
And then a shot rang out
as Tom missed John and hit Eve's arm.
It knocked Eve back toward the tracks.
John turned around to see
the steady gun, then turned again
to grab Evonne and flee.
Three more shots and . . .

This was a very exciting poem to write, full of imagery and twists and turns. Once I started, I had no idea what my muse had in mind.

The final ending was a surprise to me, too. Check it out in my anthology entitled "Enlightened Journeys," coming out in 2014.